RADIANT MORNING SUN SILHOUETTES ENGELMANN SPRUCE IN COLORADO'S SAN JUAN MOUNTAINS.

America's

Prepared by the Special Publications Division
National Geographic Society, Washington, D. C.

ROBED IN AUTUMN GOLD, QUAKING ASPENS GLOW IN THE CRISP AIR OF THE ROCKIES.

Wild Woodlands

AMERICA'S WILD WOODLANDS

Contributing Authors: WILLIAM HOWARTH,
 JANE R. MCCAULEY, H. ROBERT MORRISON,
 JENNIFER C. URQUHART, MERRILL WINDSOR
Contributing Photographers: PAUL CHESLEY,
 MIKE CLEMMER, STEVEN C. KAUFMAN,
 TIM THOMPSON
Illustrations by ALAN SINGER

Published by THE NATIONAL GEOGRAPHIC SOCIETY
GILBERT M. GROSVENOR, *President*
MELVIN M. PAYNE, *Chairman of the Board*
OWEN R. ANDERSON, *Executive Vice President*
ROBERT L. BREEDEN, *Vice President,*
 Publications and Educational Media

Prepared by THE SPECIAL PUBLICATIONS DIVISION
DONALD J. CRUMP, *Editor*
PHILIP B. SILCOTT, *Associate Editor*
WILLIAM L. ALLEN, *Senior Editor*
MARY ANN HARRELL, *Consulting Editor*

Staff for this Book
PAUL D. MARTIN, *Managing Editor*
JOHN G. AGNONE, *Picture Editor*
JODY BOLT, *Art Director*
BARBARA A. PAYNE, *Project Coordinator*
 and Senior Researcher
MONIQUE F. EINHORN, *Researcher*
BARBARA MACLEOD, *Research Assistant*
WILLIAM HOWARTH, JANE R. MCCAULEY,
 H. ROBERT MORRISON, BARBARA A. PAYNE,
 JENNIFER C. URQUHART, MERRILL WINDSOR,
 Picture Legend Writers
ELIZABETH ANN BRAZEROL,
 PAMELA BLACK TOWNSEND, *Editorial Assistants*
CAROL ROCHELEAU CURTIS, *Illustrations Assistant*
PAM CASTALDI, *Design Assistant*

Engraving, Printing, and Product Manufacture
ROBERT W. MESSER, *Manager*
GEORGE V. WHITE, *Production Manager*
MARY A. BENNETT, *Production Project Manager*
MARK R. DUNLEVY, DAVID V. SHOWERS,
 GREGORY STORER, GEORGE J. ZELLER, JR.,
 Assistant Production Managers
JULIA F. WARNER, *Production Staff Assistant*
DIANNE T. CRAVEN, LORI E. DAVIE,
 MARY ELIZABETH DAVIS, ANN DI FIORE,
 EVA A. DILLON, ROSAMUND GARNER,
 BERNADETTE L. GRIGONIS,
 VIRGINIA W. HANNASCH, NANCY J. HARVEY,
 JOAN HURST, ARTEMIS S. LAMPATHAKIS,
 KATHERINE R. LEITCH, CLEO E. PETROFF,
 VIRGINIA A. WILLIAMS, ERIC WILSON,
 Staff Assistants
CATHE WARFORD, *Indexer*

EDWARD SCHELL

CRESTED DWARF IRIS BRIGHTENS THE WOODLAND FLOOR IN TENNESSEE'S CHEROKEE

NATIONAL FOREST. HARDCOVER: CLINGING TO A PINECONE, A CHICKADEE FEEDS UPSIDE DOWN. ILLUSTRATION BY ARTHUR AND ALAN SINGER.

PACIFIC
FORESTS

ROCKY
MOUNTAIN
FORESTS

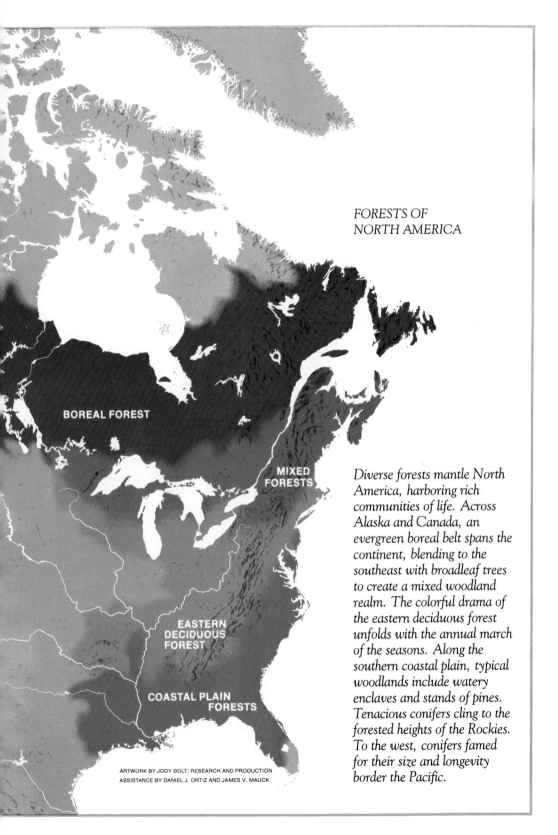

FORESTS OF
NORTH AMERICA

BOREAL FOREST

**MIXED
FORESTS**

**EASTERN
DECIDUOUS
FOREST**

**COASTAL PLAIN
FORESTS**

ARTWORK BY JODY BOLT; RESEARCH AND PRODUCTION
ASSISTANCE BY DANIEL J. ORTIZ AND JAMES V. MAUCK

*Diverse forests mantle North
America, harboring rich
communities of life. Across
Alaska and Canada, an
evergreen boreal belt spans the
continent, blending to the
southeast with broadleaf trees
to create a mixed woodland
realm. The colorful drama of
the eastern deciduous forest
unfolds with the annual march
of the seasons. Along the
southern coastal plain, typical
woodlands include watery
enclaves and stands of pines.
Tenacious conifers cling to the
forested heights of the Rockies.
To the west, conifers famed
for their size and longevity
border the Pacific.*

7

Foreword

By Robert Traver

SUGAR MAPLE
Acer saccharum

I HAVE LOVED and lived among trees all my life, for it was my good luck to have been born on the Upper Peninsula of Michigan, that treasure trove of forestland that juts into Lakes Superior, Huron, and Michigan. Some of my earliest memories of trees are of those in our iron-fenced front yard, which I so often crawled among looking for my lost teddy bear, or fell from, crying for my mother, or foraged through, recovering strayed croquet balls for my older brothers.

Especially do I recall the day I'd hit a wayward foul ball that sailed unerringly toward our side porch and on through the trees and through the sitting-room window, landing, along with most of the broken glass, on the lap of my startled mother—who at that moment was staring at the screaming headlines announcing the outbreak of the First World War.

Soon our country joined in that war; my two brothers enlisted; and my poor fisherman father, suddenly bereft of his favorite gillies, had promptly drafted me. That was how I one day found myself being whisked away on my first fishing trip. My father was taking me to his camp, grimly clutching the wheel of his old Model T Ford, which he habitually drove with all the hunched intensity of a novice taking his first roller coaster ride.

Our sandy two-rut road kept winding through dense stands of jack pine as if neither would ever end. "Look!" my father said, pointing as two deer burst from a clump of trees, leaping and bounding away like bobbing figures on a merry-go-round. Both of us fell silent as we passed through a cemetery of huge stumps, mute headstones to the giant white pines that had stood there before I was born.

The rest of our trip seemed lost in a whirl of trees and more bounding deer and swooping hawks and a lone circling eagle. "Look," my father again said. Far in the distance loomed a vast range of forested hills, densely covered with trees of so many shades that the scene looked more like some gigantic mural painted by an inspired or drunken artist. "Locals call 'em the Green Hills," said my father.

Soon we were crawling past the first in a series of beaver ponds, my father busily pointing out the dimpling trout, the flying ducks, and that thatched beaver lodge over there—all to the accompaniment of a steady chorus of shrilling frogs. As we passed the last pond I felt my spine tingling as I listened to the haunting, wavering call of an unseen loon.

Then came the slow crawl through a deep forest of mixed trees, my father explaining the differences between the leafy and needled ones, pausing to stare at a gigantic leaning white pine that had somehow survived a bolt of lightning— "Tough cookies, trees," he said. A final pause while we got out to look up at a pair of nesting eagles, each wearing a freshly laundered white bonnet. Then a sudden bend, and my father pulled up in a grassy clearing in which stood a lone log cabin with a steep tar-paper roof. "We're here, son," he said. "Grab the water pails."

I emerged from that bygone weekend permanently hooked on both trees and trout. In many ways, as I look back, I probably also reached the peak of arboreal innocence. For things began to change after that. The call of loons and of shrilling frogs became lost in the wail of saws and

rumbling trucks. Among the earliest casualties were those once endless miles of jack pines, soon followed by those looming green hills: The last autumn I ever saw them they were still there in all their wild variety of color and species; the next a sprawling tangle of stumps and slashings and dented plastic jugs.

As the wild pace accelerated I began asking myself more and more questions: Granted that we must harvest some of our forests, why do we fail to have countrywide policies about cutting, replanting, and slash-control? How can we land men on the moon and not save our elms or stem the spread of virulent chain-saw disease? Is our world becoming hopelessly divided into two kinds of people: those who love trees and those who love logs?

This book raises more than a ray of hope. It shows what's being done, and what remains to be done, to save our wild woodlands. Perhaps its most encouraging feature is the knowledge it gives of all the people who really care—the dedicated individuals and groups toiling not only to save our forests but to spread them round the country. It's a book that gives me hope to be around to see how it all pans out, a book to keep and cherish. Finally, it's a book concerned with the importance of being earnest about the forests we all need to sustain the web of life upon this already precarious planet.

Robert Traver is the pen name of John D. Voelker, author of numerous short stories and novels, including the best-seller Anatomy of a Murder. *A former Michigan Supreme Court justice, he still maintains a camp in the woods of the Upper Peninsula.*

FOLLOWING PAGES: FOG DRIFTS ABOVE THE GREAT SMOKIES IN TENNESSEE.

SISSE BRIMBERG

Woodland details highlight forest life in Alabama's Sipsey Wilderness. Vines of common greenbrier (above) produce small berries sometimes eaten by birds. Fallen leaves crown a royal fern (below, left) and mosslike filmy ferns (right). A little acorn (below, right) begins its journey to becoming a mighty white oak. All weave a complex tapestry, the forest ecosystem.

PAGES 14-15: *Young visitor marvels at a champion in Oregon's Klootchy Creek Park. With a girth greater than 50 feet, this 216-foot Sitka spruce ranks as the largest of its kind.*

13

The Bright Mosaic

By *William Howarth*
Photographs by *Steven C. Kaufman*

PAPER BIRCH
Betula papyrifera

ON THIS MORNING in early April, the woods are cold and damp. Wind gusts shudder in the treetops; branches creak and moan. The scene is grim, barren, apparently lifeless. Yet my companion is excited: "You can easily read a forest," Henry Horn says, "and here we have a little bit of everything."

He is not exaggerating. My journey through the northeastern woodlands could not begin in a better classroom than the Institute Woods of Princeton, New Jersey. We are standing on a natural crossroads, between north-south climate zones and the east-west fall line, where coastal plain meets upland piedmont. Here southern dogwood blooms beside northern birch; a low-lying grove of pines may flank higher stands of oaks.

A professor of biology at Princeton University, Dr. Horn is an authority on trees and their succession, or family history. Pines and oaks represent the two major tree groups, conifer and broadleaf—also called evergreen and deciduous, softwood and hardwood. Conifers are cone-shaped trees with spiny needles; broadleafs grow in spreading, rounded forms. Every autumn, broadleafs shed; "deciduous" is from the Latin, to fall off.

Broadleaf and conifer form the bright mosaic of mixed forest that arcs across the Northeast, from Atlantic coast to the Great Lakes. The region abounds with hundreds of plant and animal species, with millions of people. We have lived here for centuries, using the forest heavily. Our virgin timber is mostly gone. Disease has ravaged prime hardwoods, such as chestnut and elm. And yet the trees endure. Forest acreage has increased since the early 1900s, when wood was a principal fuel and building material for many.

Henry takes me on a brisk walking tutorial. Below is the forest floor, above the canopy. Understory and overstory, foot and crown—within these zones live the forest competitors. "The trees compete for soil, nutrients, water, and light. In this rich, moist soil, whoever gets the most light wins." He glances at a young beech, shooting past a maple. "That's a losing situation. The maple has had it."

This dormant scene in April actually conceals a breakneck race. "The season begins early, down near the ground," Henry remarks. "Those shrubs and ferns are photosynthesizing like mad." They grow when they can, converting light into food before the dark canopy closes. He kicks at a beech stump, bristling with new sprouts. "I call these sons of beeches." I detect his twinkle. "They pop up from stumps, roots, even bark cells. One parent tree can populate a whole acre."

While sprouting, a tree also buds and leafs, spreading out its solar panels to soak up radiant energy. Each new part springs from its elders, in the V- or Y-branching that must be nature's favorite pattern. Roots branch, as do limbs, twigs, leaves, and leaf veins. By dividing, the tree seeks to conquer, extending its forces to grow more dominant.

The end of this race is a beginning, making seeds that will generate new life. And here the principle of succession arises. Many seeds cannot germinate immediately beneath their parent trees, which are using up light, food, and space for roots. Seeds must find new turf; thus pines rise beneath oaks, oaks sprout amid pines. Generations of species succeed one another, in slow, alternating waves.

Henry dashes this image of harmony by pointing to a swath of trees, felled by wind in 1976: "Nature is timbering all the time." The dank smell of rot arises. Dead wood provides food for bacteria, as well as for insects—which in turn feed reptiles and birds. This chain of life satisfies the biologist. "The best competitors may win," he notes. "But every winner must contend with many accidents of history."

We are walking on historic ground, near the Institute for Advanced Study. Along these forest paths once strolled Einstein and Oppenheimer, fathers of the nuclear age. Yet the Institute Woods have their own patriarchs. Henry leads me to the oldest trees, seven acres of beech that he dates to 1727. How does he know, without felling the trees?

He produces a bright metal tool, T-shaped and corkscrew. "My increment borer. A painless form of extraction." From a nearby red maple he quickly pulls a pale, moist core. "This partial sample suggests that the tree's age is 65 years." We see more than 40 bands of growth, and five layers: heartwood and sapwood, cambium, inner and outer bark. Wood is the tree's bony frame, cambium its growing tissue, bark the protective skin. Young layers form an arterial system, passing water up from roots, food down from leaves.

A tree has many unseen powers. Its root system spreads far underground, matching the network of branches above. Inside the bark are enormous pressures, lifting water against gravity. Henry wipes healing lanolin on the core and replaces it. "A busy time in there—adding new wood, moving sugar. Sap's on the rise. They'll be tapping maples up north."

On the telephone Harold Howrigan of Fairfield, Vermont, wastes no words. Still boiling for sugar? "A-yup." When does a day's work end? "Dark." By noon the next day I am collecting sap with Harold's son, Mike, and a hired man—appropriately named Dick Sweet. Our sap wagon bumps across fields and enters sugar bush, the forested hillsides. Each maple tree wears an anklet of five-gallon buckets, lidded to keep out rain and snow.

"It's mud season now," says Mike, "time to bring in Vermont gold." He's referring to maple syrup, one of the most labor-intensive crops in America. Sap drips slowly into the buckets, a few ounces each hour. Five gallons may take three days. The wagon tub holds 150 gallons, which will boil down to less than four gallons of syrup.

The work is pleasant but tiring. When thirsty, I drink the cold, thin sap. Some buckets are brimming full, others scant or dry. "There's lots of theories about sap rise," Mike reports. "Mostly, it takes cold nights and warm days to get a good run." Rapid freeze shocks the trees, forcing the sap quickly upward. During a thaw the sap is free to flow. But constant warm weather stops the flow and promotes bacteria that gradually plug tapholes. "Dad says if it's warm enough to hear frogs, the season is pretty well gone."

At the sugarhouse, Harold Howrigan presides over a wood-fired evaporator. The air is steaming moist, with a distinct maple tang. Using a flat metal scoop, Harold constantly skims the hot sap as it slowly cooks to a thick amber. "Vermont Fancy has to be a nice light shade, with 86 percent pure sugar." In the window, a row of sample bottles provides him with quality standards.

Many sugar farmers now boost production by collecting sap with pumps and tubing, but Harold prefers his traditional buckets: "You have to lay and collect tubing; otherwise squirrels or mice riddle it

with holes." As he talks, family members bustle around the sugarhouse. Everyone helps at this season, often around the clock. "It's a good life," Harold says. "Other farming is dull compared to this."

He checks the fire, then tosses in chunks of dry oak. The Howrigans spend three months each year cutting firewood. They improve their woodlot by removing diseased or stunted trees, leaving a forest that will continue to provide both maple sap and hardwood fuel. Six weeks of boiling have burned up 150 cords. Harold muses, "I could have sold that wood in Burlington for eighty dollars a cord."

In Burlington the wood dealers have a hungry new customer, the McNeil Generating Station. Project engineer John Irving leads me through this nine-story power plant, one of the world's biggest wood-fired boilers. He explains how fire will produce hot gases, changing water into superheated steam. The steam will generate 50 megawatts of electricity, while radiant heat warms the building.

This loop of forces begins with lowly wood chips, the sort used in garden mulch. We peer into a hundred-ton storage bin, where the air smells of strong vinegar. "Stay here and your eyes will begin to smart," warns John. "Wood is 40 percent volatile material." Also volatile is the question of how wood-chipping will affect Vermont's forests. The plant needs a billion pounds of chips a year. Will the woods grow as fast as McNeil burns them?

Near Lake Champlain, Marvin Tallman shows me a stand of "junk" pine he is chipping. "They're not straight, stout trees, the sort you'd take for logs. These have rotten centers and weevils in the crown." Yes, but left alone this "junk" would fall, rot, and feed a natural energy system. When trees become a harvest crop, human values take over. I watch the crew run its no-hands operation: sheared, skidded, and chipped, a 70-year old pine becomes mulch in seconds. Marvin admires this speed: "Not like the old days, when any Jack with an ax was a logger."

"Go, Liz, nail it! Come on, Ellen, more back! Tech-nique, Tech-nique, Tech-nique!" A crowd chants in rhythm as crosscut saws bite through cants—squared logs— of pine. The sawyers are both Jacks and Jills; their T-shirts read Colby, Dartmouth, Penn State. At the Intercollegiate Woodsmen's Weekend, students are competing in old-time lumberjack skills. For two days they carve canoe paddles, toss lengths of pulpwood, climb 32-foot poles and bow-saw the tops. Winners earn a Woodsmen's Cup, and the losers have a good time.

The host this year is Paul Smith's College, lying in the Adirondack Mountains of northern New York. Paul Smith's regards its woodsmen as athletes and is proud of the winning dynasty they have established. The team has a vigorous coach in Gould Hoyt, who at 63 can outpace many of his trainees.

Today Gould is everywhere at once, making repairs and coaching loudly. He takes a few moments to reflect on his work in forestry education. "After graduate school, I worked as a lumberjack in the lower Hudson Valley. At another job, with the state conservation department, I owned four suits and sat inside all day. So I quit and came to Paul Smith's in 1952. Here, I can put on snowshoes and take students out to the trees in our silviculture plots."

Gould has trained members of the forestry club to use skills and hand tools now largely outmoded by machinery. He fiercely defends this program: "Students need to become good workers. They have to think and produce on their own, without machines. You can take pride in being able to chop or saw well with your hands."

Here in the Adirondacks, I am in one of America's oldest forest preserves, "forever kept as wild forest lands," according to an 1894 amendment to the New York Constitution. But in fact the region has long been a center for logging and tourism. In the Adirondacks, a "camp" is often a sumptuous log cabin.

At Blue Mountain Lake, the Adirondack Museum commemorates this history of rustic splendor. Director Craig Gilborn gives me a tour of some monuments to our wooden age: carved stagecoaches and sleighs, graceful Adirondack guide boats with ribs of spruce root.

Also displayed is rustic furniture, built by local craftsmen from mountain hardwood. "The carpenters had no pattern books," Craig notes, "so each piece is unique, not made on an assembly line." Rustic chairs and tables retain the properties of the original wood. Bark, roots, and knotty curves interrupt the formal lines. "Not everyone likes the style. Rustic is rough and unpeeled. To me, it's a welcome relief from Formica."

I ask if the museum has any modern concerns, and Craig leads me to a large bus. Inside is an exhibit on acid rain, the region's major environmental problem. "We plan to visit campsites, schools, festivals—anywhere a crowd will listen. This bus was once a bookmobile, so it's used to carrying ideas."

Since 1900 air pollution has increased atmospheric acidity, which can be deposited on thin mountain soil. Lacking adequate neutralizers, the soil and surface water become acidic. The acid releases potentially toxic aluminum from the soil. When this aluminum enters streams or ponds it can kill fish and other aquatic life. Predators up the food chain starve or leave. A forest without loons and otters can hardly keep forever wild.

Today many of the Adirondacks' ponded waters are virtually dead, where no fish swim at all. Red spruce is also dying; studies suggest that airborne pollutants harm the needles and root hairs. Without stronger air quality controls, more damage may lie ahead. Prevailing winds eventually sweep pollutants northeast, toward New Hampshire and the White Mountains.

As I stand in the wilds of New Hampshire on a bright June day, the Great Gulf

WHITE SPRUCE
Picea glauca

Trail looks inviting. But above me Mount Washington still broods in winter. The tallest peak in New England has some of the world's worst weather. Cold winds sweep across its rugged face; at the 6,288-foot summit, snow has fallen every month of the year.

For every thousand feet that I ascend, the tempèrature drops three and a third degrees, as though I had driven some 200 miles north. By noon I will pass Quebec; the peak will resemble Labrador. I will also journey through a plant succession, going from mixed broadleaf-conifer to the treeless alpine world. At the summit lies New Hampshire as it was 10,000 years ago, after the last glaciers retreated.

Few hikers are out this early; for a companion I talk to my small tape recorder. "I've gone about a mile, and mostly I see ash or maple in the lower parts. . . . At 1,800 feet, I'm finding lady's slippers and moist beds of fern. The maple and birch trees are really big, over 80 feet tall, but balsam fir and spruce are taking over. . . . Saw three snowshoe hares, as big as cats, playing tag in the underbrush. Springtime, I guess."

The Great Gulf Wilderness is a 5,552-acre basin, hollowed by glacial scouring and stream-cut down its middle. Only at 3,000 feet can I finally see this shape, as the trail rises steeply and trees grow short. Two-thirds are conifers now; the air has the sharp scent of spruce. Hearing the high, sweet call of a white-throated sparrow, I feel at last in the heart of wild New England.

My tape reels on: "I can see the top, but I'm facing a headwall of rubble, going straight up. The trail is a string of painted blazes. . . . All bare rock at 4,800 feet. The last trees are birch and balsam fir, stunted to shrub level. . . . Just sedges and some ground plants at the top. . . . Boy, feel that WIND!"

At the Mount Washington Observatory, Greg Gordon is not impressed by tonight's breeze: "Gusting to 91 miles per hour. About right for June." The world's highest recorded wind, 231 miles per hour, occurred here in April 1934. Fifty years later, Greg and others check the mountain's weather every three hours, day and night. In winter they come up the auto road on snow tractors; the daredevils sometimes go home on skis or even sleds. Though he has a remote office, Greg enjoys his mountain-top perch: "It's the *highest* paying job in New England."

If vegetation is scarce up here, enter-prise is not. The summit is both a state park (souvenir shop, cafeteria, office, storage shed) and business complex (mu-seum, radio-TV relay transmitter, cog railway, auto road). Down in the Great Gulf, I hiked through national forest—managed by the Forest Service—on a trail maintained by volunteers from the Appa-lachian Mountain Club (AMC).

A day's hike with Ned Therrien and Steve Rice tells me more about this net-work of interests. As representatives of the Forest Service and AMC, they are seeing if an old loggers' road can serve as a backcountry trail. Steve describes a long history of such cooperation: "The AMC first explored and mapped this region, then strongly promoted creation of the eastern national forest system. Our goal is to preserve wild lands for recreation. We want to see forests managed for the public benefit."

Ned concurs: "Federal management of forests makes good sense in the East. Higher populations mean heavier use. We are within a day's drive of 60 million people. But the forest recovers quickly in this favorable climate, so we can support both recreation and logging. We can af-ford to produce large, high-quality hard-woods, which may need 80 to 120 years to mature."

Recently, with federal budget cut-backs, this goodwill has been tested. The Forest Service now spends less money to repair trails, more time in pursuit of log-ging contracts—which gives AMC mem-bers the jitters. Yet both organizations are still working together to acquire land for the national forest.

Steve predicts that our trail will be "rough." Hours later I agree, dubbing us the Appalachian Mud Club. For miles we have splashed along creeks and through dense undergrowth. Black flies swarm over us, merciless in their surgery. Ned of-fers me some insect repellent; Steve lends a netted helmet. He is a patient traveler: "Black flies come with this country. You'll find them all the way to Maine."

From Kidney Pond I can see Mount Katahdin, but my eyes are on the shoreline. A young bull moose wades there, feeding on green wil-low shoots. I dip my paddle slightly, and the canoe glides forward. Thirty yards, fif-teen, ten. Finally he lifts his head. For a minute we study each other. Behind me a loon call rises in long, keening wails. I look for the singer, then back to the moose. He has slipped away.

Moose and loon are synonymous with these northern woods, and Baxter State Park still has plenty of both animals. This wilderness preserve, 314 square miles of north-central Maine, vigorously protects its wildlife. In a letter written in 1945, the park's donor, former Governor Percival Baxter, deplored what he called "the trappings of unpleasant civilization": bill-boards, hotels, hot dog stands, and air-planes. Yet the governor was not rigid. In the 1950s, he bought additional land for a forestry management area, which works to determine how controlled hunting and logging affect the preserve.

Baxter Park has its own set of forestry goals, as director Buzz Caverly explains: "We won't cut trees if that threatens our clean water or rare plants. During and af-ter logging, we'll maintain campgrounds in the harvested zones. They will keep open northern sections of the park to visi-tors and reduce pressure on the south." But pressure has also come to the park from an insect pest that infests most of northern Maine.

Near Presque Isle, state entomologist Henry Trial opens his palm to show me the enemy: a small, rusty-brown larva known as the spruce budworm. "Sixth instar," Henry notes. "That's the stage of growth when they feed heavily and are agile. This one is into the male flowers. He'll destroy the reproductive system and then the top branches, where growth is crucial."

Budworm is always among us, and at intervals it reaches epidemic infestations. It then kills trees, creating a fire hazard for the entire forest. Even at lower infestation levels, the insects can retard tree growth, which means less profit for loggers. "And less jobs for Maine, less wood for America," adds Henry. "Spruce-fir pulp makes high-quality coated paper, of the type sold to the National Geographic Society."

I think of my readers, some of whom may object to wide-scale pest control. Aren't insects a natural hazard, like other crop diseases? Tom Rumpf, Maine's director of budworm control, concedes, "Sure, nature could solve this problem. If we let the worms eat up their food supply, they'd starve to death. But we can't afford to wait. Demand for forest products is growing. We need to have a supply of healthy, full-grown trees. All things considered, it's better to spray."

Death for the budworm rains down from an air squadron that flies at dawn from Presque Isle. The pilots man stub-winged Polish Dromaders and the large four-props of World War II, DC-4s. At 5 a.m. I watch a Dromader skimming the treetops at 50 feet to lay down spray. Above is a guide plane, using an electronic system to plot the kill exactly. On command, spray booms pulse on and off, sparing buffer zones near water and farms. A final pass and the radio crackles: "Let's go home. We're out of juice."

Many citizen groups in Maine fear that juice. The chemicals Zectran and Matacil can be indiscriminately lethal. A bacterial spray, Bt, destroys budworms but can also kill butterflies and moths occupying the same trees. Dick Dyer, spokesman for the project, says the risks are limited. "We run the largest, best-controlled forest spraying program in the U. S., at no cost to taxpayers. Landowners pay for this service on a voluntary basis. It comes down to this: Who's going to harvest timber, Maine or the worms?"

At Pinkham Lumber, one of the largest sawmills in eastern America, Randy Caron worries about his timber. We are standing in several acres of cut logs, stacked in sloping piles. "That's a one-month supply for our production line," he says. "The logging camps aren't operating yet because of spring floods, and we've got to have logs soon."

Inside the mill, high-speed saws are slicing logs like so many sticks of butter. Sawyers run computerized consoles, pushing buttons to set the saws and aligning logs with laser beams. "Every operator has hands-on control," Randy notes. They use the old hand tools as well: When a log gets jammed, out comes a spiked picaroon to help it along.

A gentler impulse guides the hands of craftsmen at Thos. Moser, Cabinetmakers, a respected furniture studio in New Gloucester. Tom Moser grows eloquent as he rubs the smooth surface of a harvest table: "I'm always discovering something new about wood. It has grain, like a piece of leather; it has lift and give, even a personality." In his large workshop, craftsmen shape spindled chairs and sturdy benches. The forms are simple and functional, inspired by Shaker designs.

Moser seems to share the Shakers' spirit of devotion. "We have had our fill of being a throwaway society. To me, wood is a refuge—even a salvation." Does he have a favorite wood? "Cherry, because it goes on working for years. It oxidizes and takes on a warm, deep color." He gives a light rap with his knuckles. Does the cherry grow here in Maine? "No, it comes from the Alleghenies, out in western Pennsylvania."

The Allegheny Plateau runs across northern Pennsylvania, rolling country with peaks that are remnants of a single uplifted mass of sedimentary rock now eroded away. The forests on the Allegheny Plateau have also changed dramatically with time. Pine went first, for construction; then tanning factories stripped the hemlock for its tannin-rich bark; finally railroads came and loggers cut the hardwood stands of beech, maple, oak, ash, and cherry.

In the Tionesta Natural Area, a 4,000-acre remnant of primeval woods, the long, slow process of species succession has gone undisturbed. Here I can walk through nature's ultimate climax forest, passing from hemlocks in the low, wet ground to beeches on the dry uplands. My hiking companion, Dave Marquis, lists some hidden virtues: "You'll find no poison ivy here, no ticks, and not many snakes." He might be describing paradise, yet the woods here are heading for trouble.

Beneath the great trees we should find a healthy understory of seedlings and herbs. "There's plenty of beech, but we've not seen hemlock reproduction in 30 years. Also no shrubs; just lots of hay-scented and New York ferns. The ferns release a natural herbicide, keeping other growth down."

In a nearby area, we find that the major culprits are four- and two-legged. White-tailed deer have browsed the understory into oblivion. With abundant food, the deer population booms, and so do the guns of hunters. "Pennsylvania has the largest deer harvest in the U. S.," says Dave. "That supports a tourist industry, but the deer kill off ash and cherry, our two best hardwoods. So we have a biological problem that is also political in nature."

As research project leader of the Forestry Sciences Laboratory at Warren, Dr. Marquis has to promote the coexistence of deer and trees. Many varieties of trees normally survive browsing and

grow out of reach, but an excessive deer population retards this process or halts it entirely. The deer tend to pass over beech, which sprouts quickly from the roots of parent trees. The forest regenerates as a monoculture, lacking variety. Dave points to a grove of mature beech: "Those are even-aged trees, with little below to replace them. The understory lacks cover or food for wildlife, like grouse or rabbits."

The solution lies in adjusting both populations, increasing the seedlings and reducing the deer. Dave promotes shelterwood cutting, a process that first opens the canopy to establish large numbers of seedlings, then later removes the overstory so new trees can shoot up. Deer face the same process of thinning. Crowded areas will be cleared. Fewer animals will starve in winter and the survivors will be healthy.

"Come on, Eleven, you've got some company." Nancy Tilghman is calling a white-tailed doe. "She likes men better than women, but best of all are Life Savers." The doe's real savior may be Dr. Tilghman, a research wildlife biologist at Warren who is searching for a favorable balance between trees and deer.

The next day she takes me to her outdoor lab, 160 acres of fenced woodlot. "Let's see if we can dial up a deer." She fiddles with a radio receiver and rotates its antenna. "There's Red, heading our way. She likes to see visitors." Deer 134 soon appears, ear flapping with a bright red tag. Red lives alone on 64 acres, simulating ten deer per square mile. Nearby are four deer on 32 acres, or 80 per square mile. The difference in forest is obvious: "Few seedlings, with little variety, in the high-deer area—and all of them are short." Nancy is not tall, but she towers over these trees.

Later we sit on a slope beneath Minister Ridge, in the shade of a young pin cherry. That's the only tree in this clearcut, thanks to a surrounding fence. "Without the fence, this whole area would be nothing more than a fern meadow." Is the answer to kill off some of the deer? "As a scientist, I have to say yes. People created this monoculture, so people have to restore a more natural balance."

When I last see Dave Marquis, he is tending the forest with a computer. A program called SILVAH takes data from landowners, then recommends a precise harvest: so much in partial thinning, much less in clear-cutting. "Faulty deer management followed by clear-cuts led to our problems. So today we have to handle both deer and trees more cautiously." Was the greatest clear-cut here? "No, it was just as widespread in Michigan."

D riving north from Detroit, I can see the woods of a secondary succession, mostly birch-aspen and assorted pines: white, Norway, and jack. A century ago the white pine dominated Michigan, crowding its sky with tall pagoda forms. Legends are told of squirrels traveling miles without leaving pine branches, of pine pollen on the horizon in clouds of golden smoke.

Today only small, scattered stands of old-growth white pine survive. All the rest has gone under to the ax, saw, or fire. Forty-nine acres of virgin white pines lie protected within 9,672-acre Hartwick Pines State Park near Grayling. "More trees here were lost to fire than cutting," says Wendell Hoover, park interpreter. "Spring fires destroyed seeds and young trees as well as mature pines, thus preventing regeneration."

He leads a group of visitors into the grove of pines. People look up—and quiet down, hushed by the sight of life this big and old. At the Monarch Pine, Wendell announces: "This tree is over 300 years old. It stands 155 feet high, and the circumference at the base is nearly 12 feet. You're looking at a five-room house."

We can't seem to build without tearing down. This melancholy thought occurs to me at some park exhibits on

Michigan's logging heyday, 1870-1910. Old photographs tell the story: logs in rivers and on lakes, logs skidded over ice on sledges, and in summer slung beneath "Big Wheels," carts with ten-foot wheels made in Michigan and sold worldwide. Big Wheels doubled the logging season, and so big pines went their way.

At the western edge of Crawford County I find a graveyard of white pine stumps, cut around 1900. They resemble gray and weathered sculpture, surrounded by patches of tall, nodding hawkweed. Some have five-foot diameters; when cut, they were more than 300 years old. A few rise above my head, probably measuring the deep snows of winter. All seem to be waiting, in silent reproach to those who rarely stop today.

At dawn I go in search of another waning species, the Kirtland's warbler. Sunshine is warming the wild roses; no wind stirs the jack pines along this sandy road. Conditions are ideal to spot the warblers, whose numbers have declined to just over 400. And all about me I can hear . . . the barking rattle of machine-gun fire.

Ron Hicks nods: "National Guard. They come from all over the Midwest for summer maneuvers. I've seen tanks and trucks on this road while we were spotting warblers." A biologist from California, Ron was working in Michigan for the U. S. Fish and Wildlife Service. That's less strange than the fact that one of America's rarest warblers nests in an artillery range. Of course the warblers arrived first, choosing north-central Michigan because it meets their strict nesting requirements: dense stands of young jack pines, branches touching, on well-drained sand. Such conditions are found here in a 60-mile radius, parts of 12 counties. The nesting ground concludes a long journey for the warblers, which winter in the Bahamas.

Ron locates a male bird and we take turns at the scope, to catch his morning show. Not all rare birds are beautiful, but this one is a jewel. He wears pale yellow on his breast, folds black-edged wings against blue-gray sides. His song is constant, a slurred series of notes with tail flicking time. Overhead, a drab olive helicopter stutters by.

"The Guard is cooperative," Ron says. "They avoid the area, and their mortar rounds and flares also start fires, which sometimes help the birds." Fires actually promote jack pine, for heat melts the resin that seals the cones, releasing seeds. As my friend Henry Horn says, nature is timbering all the time. Fires that destroyed white pine have helped regenerate jack pine, and so kept warblers alive.

Today northern Michigan is growing less wild. More land is opening for the building of homes. Fires that break out are quickly suppressed. Such changes threaten the warbler's survival. "We are doing what we can in Michigan," says Ron, "but our recovery plan also touches other areas. The bird needs protection in the Bahamas and new nesting grounds up here. Some good areas may lie farther north, in Minnesota and Canada."

Minnesota is the southern limit of the vast boreal forest, which runs north to the treeless tundra of Canada. Long, cold winters dominate this country. The growing season is short, and soil remains stony thin. Most deciduous trees cannot survive here, save for hardy species such as birch, aspen, and ash. Conifers rule the boreal forest, rimming its glacial lakes and streams with an unbroken mantle of green.

Because the forest is so dense, most early travel was by water. Indians journeyed about in canoes, strong light vessels they built of root and bark. Throughout the Great Lakes region they developed water routes, later followed by French voyageurs. They followed the beaver, source of the great North American fur trade.

Near Kabetogama Lake, in Voyageurs National Park, I watch a beaver repair his dam. For an hour he has made

BLACK WALNUT
Juglans nigra

long journeys back to a coppice of aspens. He cuts a branch, then tows it downstream. Underwater, he accurately packs the branch in a crevice.

The pond above this dam holds a lodge and food pile, two masses of brushwood. The shoreline is stripped, and each day the beaver's journey for timber grows longer. Eventually he will leave to build a pond elsewhere. The untended dam may hold for years, retaining water for ducks and fish. And the beaver labors on, building a world far beyond his modest needs.

"I want you to imagine the hills covered with red and white pine, trees a hundred feet tall and over three feet in diameter. Then imagine the hills as bare, the lake surface covered with logs. That was the scene here in 1910, when the Virginia & Rainy Lake Lumber Company was cutting wood for the largest pine mill in the world." Seasonal naturalist Chuck Campbell gestures at the shoreline forest, which is dense now but has little pine.

Chuck guides boat trips for visitors through the complex maze of lake and forest in Voyageurs National Park. He occasionally consults maps as we thread a course between islands and bays along the Canada-U. S. boundary. Voyageurs established this line with their canoes; engineers spanned it with three dams to raise the water levels.

At Kettle Falls, water is rushing over a spillway, going east into Canada. "Paper companies need water upstream," Chuck explains, "and a dam at this point can raise over eight feet of water." The American and Canadian lakes are reservoirs, with closely regulated levels. Seasonal fluctuations would be a more natural state, meeting the habitat needs of wild rice, shorebirds, and spawning fish. "The local fishing fleet used to catch and ship 3,500 pounds a week," Chuck says. "We'll not see those numbers again."

At times it seems more fishermen than fish now fill these waters, supporting the many private resorts and camps clustered on the lakeshores. Both the tourist business and national park hope to grow while remaining allies. Voyageurs Park is young, established in 1975. Its mission is to preserve this region while allowing for controlled public use. It also studies how the region has changed, largely through human disturbance. Research indicates that the area needs careful management to become wild again.

Glen Cole, park biologist, recites the diminished inventory: "We lost elk and caribou to hunting. Logging led to a drop in the porcupine and pine marten. Dams have affected beaver, muskrat, loon, and the two best fish, walleye and northern pike. And as our deer herds have dwindled, predators such as the wolf, coyote, fox, and lynx have also declined." Plans are under way to correct these imbalances, but recovery will be slow. Meanwhile, the boundary of prime wildlife habitat has edged north, into Ontario.

In the summers when I was growing up, my family took vacations at places we called The Lake. We lived in tents or in small cabins, rose in the early mornings to fish for bass and pike. On long afternoons we hunted frogs, which looked unhappy to be cast as bait. After supper we built log fires and talked into the night. The Lake was always north, in conifer forest country. For the past 20 years that place has been northwest Ontario, on Sunset Point.

To go there, I have crossed the border and driven north for hours, along a highway built for logging trucks. Nothing breaks the forest: no signs or houses, no services for a hundred miles. Most of the region is Crown land, open for recreation or licensed for logging. Near Sioux Lookout, Ontario, I swing onto the gravel roads of Ojibway Provincial Park. More miles of travel follow, by car and then boat. I am one hour from a phone, two from a doctor, four from an emergency ward. At the end of this chain sits a long rocky dike, and a log cabin facing west: Sunset Point. Thousands of dragon-flies rise to greet me, the returning summer guest.

To year-round residents of Northern Ontario, this immense land is resource-rich and climate-poor. The country bursts with minerals and timber, but temperate days are relatively few. Winter sets in by October and lasts till early May. For years the region supported only a small subsistence population. But development has finally arrived on a large scale, slowly pushing north into marginal terrain. Behind this growth is Ontario's powerful Ministry of Natural Resources.

Bruce Ferguson, district forest management supervisor, explains one of the Ministry's roles: "We develop the forest at all levels—grow seed stock, improve prime species, and issue cutting licenses. The Ministry is a focal point; we try to minimize the impact of logging on other forest uses."

Yet Ojibway Park bears signs of that impact. It was selectively cut 30 years ago, then became a park. "We're not getting the ideal succession," Bruce admits. "Most of this secondary growth is balsam fir, which grows fast and then rots out. It's limby to the ground, full of eye-pokers and hard to cut. In the better-grade spruces, we have heavy budworm damage. Both species are becoming fire hazards, which of course we don't want in our camping area."

North of the camping area, a group of Ontario Junior Rangers is working to launch tomorrow's forest. The group's supervisor, Karen Mikoliew, explains: "Just outside the park, we have 20 acres of seed orchard started, nursery stock grown from the best trees in this area. We have to regenerate with improved seed and planting stock because the second generation is not coming in naturally. These are silly looking trees with exaggerated crowns, to encourage more flowers and seed production." Perhaps among these trees some tough young eccentrics will improve the forest's chances of survival.

Sixty miles northeast of Ojibway Park live two experts in survival, Wilfred and Bea Wingenroth. The Wingenroths emigrated from Germany to Canada in 1963. They took a train into the bush, then paddled north to their homesite. For more than 20 years they have lived in the wilderness by their own wits and hands. They have raised two daughters, built several log houses, and developed their own philosophy. "We want to live simply," Wilf says, "without the waste so common today."

Wilf fled north to escape civilization, but today logging operations have pushed into his homestead. "My traplines and minnow lakes took years to build up," he says, "and the pulp companies have ruined that with roads and noisy machines." No technophobe himself, Wilf owns more than 20 engines. He also has built from scratch his own snowmobile and ultralight aircraft.

But he sees these machines as aids to endure the harsh Canadian environment. "My operations are too small-scale to tip the natural balance. Wholesale timbering is another story. Soil conditions here are poor to marginal; if clear-cut with heavy machinery, the forest will never regenerate to its natural state. The Ministry is trying to protect a resource even as it promotes extraction."

As a spokesman for the Trappers Council, Wilf has earned the attention of those he criticizes. He writes papers, testifies at royal commission hearings, appears in symposia—at public expense. The man who sought solitude has become a watchman for his country.

"People think because you live on a shoestring you don't know anything. I know that if you only look after dollars, you destroy the environment—and with it goes your economic base. In the woods, there's no waste. It all recycles into blueberries. We can never manage nature. We can only use it carefully, within limits, and with utmost respect for its integrity."

*S*hades *of green and dabs of fall color brighten a northeastern forest, where coniferous and broadleaf trees intermingle. Above Squam Lake in New Hampshire (right), hikers rest on Rattlesnake Mountain—an easy 1,220-foot ascent compared with alpine Mount Washington (above), a 6,288-foot peak in the White Mountain National Forest.*

PRECEDING PAGES: Maple sap flows on a sunny March day in a 20-acre sugar bush near Whitingham, Vermont. Buckets, draft horses, and strong arms gather the thin sap for a wood-fired evaporator. In one hour, 200 gallons of sap boil down to 5 gallons of syrup.

Maple and birch blaze softly amid dark spires of spruce, fir, and pine on the road to Maine's Baxter State Park (below). North America has its flaming fall thanks to favorable weather and a large variety of deciduous trees. Fall colors emerge as sunlight wanes and nights lengthen. Green chlorophyll fades, revealing existing pigments of yellow and orange. Purple and scarlet tones, as in the red maple leaves at right, form only in fall. The maple's bright embers glow in warm sunshine, even after heavy frost.

*T*railing plumes of pesticide, a DC-4 sprays giant blocks of woodland in northern Maine to control infestations of spruce budworm (below, left). The state-run spraying program has treated more than 18 million acres of trees since 1954. Budworms prefer spruce and fir, the heart of Maine's timber crop. In larval stages the insects feed on branch tips, prime sites for tree growth and reproduction. Most of the infested trees die within five years.

Cut and stacked for drying, one-by-four-inch boards of eastern white pine await the kiln at a sawmill near New Gloucester, Maine. Large mills now rely on computers and lasers to help process lumber, but hands remain vital tools for woodsmen. At New York's Paul Smith's College (below), student sawyers compete in a two-day lumberjacking meet. The winners of this event made nine cross-cuts of eight-inch pine timber in 48.5 seconds.

*L*eaves of birch, maple, and aspen dapple a trail in Baxter State Park. Tree leaves turn and fall in a predictable sequence, according to species. This multicolored blanket will eventually decay into rich, moist soil, nourishing new generations of life. On Katahdin Stream (below), a young camper salutes the fall by launching leaf boats on a downstream journey.

JOSÉ AZEL (BOTH)

"*Not all our study animals are this friendly," says Nancy Tilghman as she greets Mildred, a 6-year-old white-tailed doe, near Smethport, Pennsylvania. To study deer browsing habits, biologist Tilghman attaches radio collars to selected animals and confines them to forest enclosures. Her study's goal: to foster a favorable balance between deer and trees. In the Allegheny Plateau region, heavy deer populations have cleared the understory of tree seedlings, leaving mostly ferns. These woodlands often fail to regenerate, and they lack the food or cover that will sustain varied wildlife.*

*S*uccess in the woods depends on light, soil, moisture—and luck. Bunchberry (right) grows profusely beneath a balsam fir in cool, damp shade but does not transplant well to home gardens. At an abandoned farmhouse in Northport, Maine (above), aspen, birch, and maple trees flourish in partial sun. Eventually the open space will give way to stands of spruce and balsam fir. The soil will then become cool, damp, and shaded—an ideal home for bunchberry.

*L*one cow moose searches Michigan's Isle Royale National Park for morning browse. Unless opened by wind or fire, dense woodlands suppress many of the shrubs and seedlings these animals require. Though wolf packs threaten moose, their main enemy is starvation.

JIM BRANDENBURG (ABOVE, LEFT AND BELOW); ANNIE GRIFFITHS (ABOVE, RIGHT)

Nature's architects, beavers shape the drainage of northern forests. In Minnesota's Superior National Forest (above), a beaver dam has created a woodland pond surrounding a lodge. At left, a beaver carries a stick in its mouth to repair the underwater base of its lodge. Though beavers feed on water lilies, their main diet consists of tree leaves and bark (far left).

FOLLOWING PAGES: Sugar maples make a last stand in Minnesota, occupying a narrow band along Lake Superior. Beyond, the largely coniferous boreal forest stretches northward.

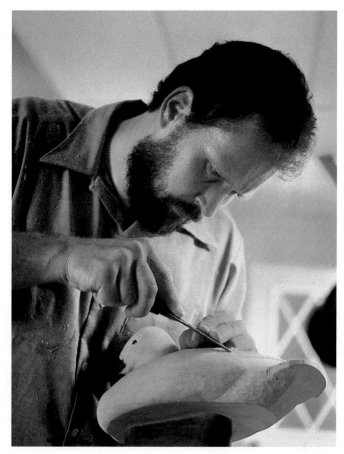

*B*ringing wood to life, award-winning bird carver Marcus Schultz shapes a canvasback duck from basswood at his studio in Denmark, Wisconsin. Schultz may spend 500 hours fashioning a single bird with chisels and gouges. His resplendent wood duck with erected head crest (left) won best-of-show honors at four international wildfowl carving competitions in 1984. Using burning pens and paint brushes, the artist painstakingly renders each natural detail, down to the most delicate feathers (below).

Hopes rising with dawn, fishermen leave Timber Edge Camps to head up Butterfly Lake near Sioux Lookout, Ontario (right). In the boreal forest of central Canada, tourism and logging form the main industries. To sustain its woodland riches, Ontario often replants clear-cuts with native species. Above, teenage Junior Rangers replant an area with black spruce seedlings. A critic of clear-cutting, wilderness advocate Wilfred Wingenroth (left) lives in the deep woods northeast of Sioux Lookout. With hearing protectors in place, he guides his boat on the Tawatinaw River. For more than 20 years, Wingenroth has fished and trapped, striving to keep his needs within the natural economy.

Highland Sanctuary

By Jennifer C. Urquhart
Photographs by Mike Clemmer

TULIP TREE
Liriodendron tulipifera

THICK SMOKE BLASTED from the locomotive's stack, 20-foot-high plumes that churned the tree branches arching above. The long wail of the whistle punctuated the chugga-chugga heartbeat of the old Shay steam engine. We had left Cass, West Virginia, the train laboring on the slow climb up 4,842-foot Bald Knob. Leaning out from a converted railcar that once carried logs along these same tracks, I could almost touch young maples, oaks, cherries, and basswoods now growing here. My ride was part of a journey that would take me to the hardwood forests of the southeastern highlands, a portion of the vast woodlands that cloaked eastern North America when the earliest settlers stepped ashore.

The forests of this region escape sharp definition. Though dominated by broadleaf trees, they are not always strictly deciduous, nor easily typed by species. In lush cove hardwood forests, for instance, perhaps 25 species may thrive with no one species predominating. If one word of description were to suffice it would have to be *variety*. The story of these woodlands is also one of devastation, and of rebirth.

At the turn of the century many of the southern Appalachian forests were networked with railroads like the Cass. The northern forests were depleted, so timbermen moved on to these less accessible trees. "If a single technological cause—oh, hell, *villain*—is to be nominated for what happened to America's forests during the late 19th century, the Shay Engine is as good a scapegoat as can be found," writes one author. The powerfully geared Shay, along with more efficient saws at the mills, spelled doom for these virgin forests. The museums at Cass display the accoutrements of early loggers—hobnail boots, crosscut saws, beat-up hats with nicks in the brim, each cut marking a day's work. Men once spent months in the woods here for $2 a day.

The Cass railroad took millions of board feet of timber out of these hills. From Black Mountain, to the southwest of Cass, I looked down into the Cranberry Wilderness, once again heavily forested. The wilderness encompasses 35,864 acres in the Monongahela National Forest in eastern West Virginia. It was hard to imagine the chaos that must have filled this now tranquil valley, the din of saws and locomotives, of metal on metal, of 400-year-old trees crashing to the ground.

This is the Allegheny region of the Appalachians. "You're saying it wrong," I was told, "the word Appalachia." A man in Richwood, near the Cranberry, finally explained. "You know, it's what Eve said to Adam—'I'll throw an apple-*at*-cha!'" Thus educated, I joined Forest Service wildlife biologist Donna Hollingsworth and her husband, Gary, one foggy June morning for a walk in the Cranberry.

We followed an old railroad bed through red spruce and yellow birch. Where the trail narrowed and skirted large boulders and rocks, Donna pointed out a striped maple. "It's called moosewood farther north. A lot of species here, particularly at higher elevations, also grow where I'm from—Wisconsin. Here's mountain maple, another northern type. They're scrawnier here. But the black cherry trees are giants." Here, too, flourished such typical southerners as sweet gums and Fraser magnolias.

Donna picked out the metallic song of a veery and then the whistling cry of a red-eyed vireo. We heard the distant staccato of a woodpecker. Donna spotted a thin wisp of down from a grouse chick. Gary, a native of the area, also picked up animal signs: Here a turkey had scratched; there a deer had browsed. "There's a stump the bears have been working over for grubs," he said.

In a way, Donna looks at a forest in terms of how it will sustain "her" wild creatures. Though the population management of the animals is actually under state control, Donna is responsible for their habitat here. She encourages food sources like fruit and nut trees. "I ask the timber specialists to favor the beeches and oaks for the mast—the acorns and nuts—they produce." Wild turkey, squirrel, and black bear abound in this deep hardwood forest. Black bear particularly. "We call the bears 'garbage guts,'" Donna said. "They'll eat anything." The region supports one of the largest bear populations in the East.

Since 1967, the Cranberry area has been a sanctuary for the bears, but the animals are hunted heavily nearby. Perhaps a hundred animals a year are killed in the national forest. Donna thinks the present estimated population of nearly 550 may not be viable at that rate of hunting. She calculates, through a complex series of formulas, that about 700 bears are needed to maintain a healthy, stable population in the Monongahela. But bears, and hunting in general, are political subjects in this region. It's difficult to get hunting quotas lowered. And, Donna thinks, timber harvesting activities may further disrupt prime bear habitat and lower the population levels.

We switched back and forth down a steep slope. Beech leaves carpeted the trail in coppery brown. We nibbled on the astringent leaves of wood sorrel. Ramps in bloom showed little white seedpods. Ramps. No other forest plant causes the stir raised by this eminently pungent member of the lily family. Spring in West Virginia brings ramp feeds at churches, fire departments, Moose clubs. It's a time, a local teacher told me, when kids who've been eating the odorous wild garlic are sent home from school. Doctors post signs: "If you've been eating ramps, go someplace else." Some say the phenomenon stems from a craving for the first greens that appear after a long winter.

Chester Carden dug up a ramp bulb with his pocketknife. "As soon as you can see 'em pushing up through the snow, you can smell 'em cooking in Richwood." I declined Chester's offer of a taste. For me one whiff was enough. A wiry outdoorsman, Chester grew up in these woods. To him, ramps represent a kind of initiation for newcomers. One time, he told me, he persuaded two young women from New York to try some before they headed home. "I figured they'd get kicked off the airplane over Washington, D. C.!" he said with a chuckle.

Before retiring, Chester spent 24 years in the Cranberry with the Forest Service. "I worked like I owned it," he said. "If I saw muddy water filling a stream, going into our water supply, I'd just walk upstream to find out where it was coming from. I've closed timber cutters down for cutting too close to the creek."

One morning we headed along a trail Chester had built around the Cranberry Glades. At first we followed an old railroad right-of-way. Chester's father had worked here on the railroad and in the logging camps. "First locomotive I ever heard in these hills," Chester told me, "I wondered how did they get that thing up on the mountain. Back when I was a kid,

they'd bring one big log out on a car—had to use dynamite to split it." We headed into deep forest, where there were a few big trees, black cherries, yellow birches, maples and beeches, left by loggers who had high-graded, or cut selectively.

Chester said he had made most of the signs that mark the trails and roads in the Cranberry. They are neat brown signs with white lettering and barbed wire on the edges. Barbed wire! Yes, apparently the bears eat the signs. Even with the wire, we found some unreadable, with great hunks bitten out. Some think the bears like the taste of the paint. I prefer to believe they just want to confuse interlopers in their territory.

Nature has healed many scars in the Cranberry—scars left by logging, erosion, and the scorching fires that swept through tinder-dry slash, often ignited by sparks from machines. But one fire in the 1930s burned with such intensity on Black Mountain that the very soil—centuries worth of rich humus—burned right down to bedrock. Standing on the high ridge where the fire had been, I could see a rocky expanse where laurel, elderberry, and blueberry bushes were making a valiant attempt in the long process of rebuilding a devastated forest.

Ramps may provide amusement for Chester Carden, but Ed Buck credits the pungent herb in part for his 82 healthy years. "The Good Lord, the outdoors, and ramps have been kind to me!" he says. Spry, with a quick wit to match, and white hair and beard worthy of Santa Claus, Ed continues to roam the woods— to fish, hunt, and trap, and to show visitors like me the wonders of the Cranberry. Ed had seen that great fire up on Black Mountain in the thirties. He was an environmentalist before it was fashionable. In Richwood High School, where he taught biology, he formed a conservation club. He has remained concerned about the welfare of the Cranberry and the whole Monongahela.

At the 750-acre Cranberry Glades

Botanical Area, adjacent to the wilderness, Ed and I cut through alders, choke-cherry, yellow birch, and shoulder-high ferns. We walked on a boardwalk that bridges the unstable glades—the local name for a bog. The glades, it is thought, began to form about 10,000 years ago following the Ice Age, which had forced many northern species southward. Uneven erosion from streams and springs trapped water in a kind of basin. Then layer upon layer of sphagnum mosses and lichens built up until the bog reached 12 feet deep in places. I gingerly stepped off the wooden walkway onto the spongy mat of plant material. Clear water quickly filled the indentation my foot made.

Plentiful precipitation, high elevation, and a cool climate combined to make this basin a refuge for northern species even after the Ice Age ended. Ed pointed out lichens—reindeer moss and old-man's beard. There were two kinds of cranberries, the largest plant measuring only eight inches high, bog rosemary, and orchids such as grass pink and rose pogonia. The glades look a lot like parts of Alaska, Ed told me, a state where he has spent some time.

Ed's full name is Edward Theodore Buck. "I'm a great admirer of Theodore Roosevelt. I'm named for him," he said. And he certainly admires the role the 26th President had in preserving and restoring America's forests.

As early as the mid-19th century, awareness was growing that America's natural resources were being diminished. By the last decades of the century, conservationists such as John Muir, Gifford Pinchot, and Teddy Roosevelt, along with other citizens, were concerned that something be done to protect our woodland areas. Finally, in 1891, Congress authorized the withdrawal of certain lands from the public domain. These forest reserves, however, were in the West, where much of the land was still under federal control. But the remaining eastern forests were under siege as well.

President Roosevelt was aware of the problem. In 1901 he wrote of the southern Appalachians: "These are the heaviest and most beautiful hard-wood forests of the continent . . . species from east and west, from north and south mingle in a growth of unparalleled richness and variety." Roosevelt understood the connection between the denuding of the land and the violent floods plaguing the East. A devastating flood, partly originating in the Monongahela watershed, swept down on Pittsburgh in 1907. This disaster and others spurred the passing of the Weeks Act in 1911, which gave the federal government, under the guise of protecting the "navigability of navigable streams," the right to acquire and rehabilitate forests and farmlands in eastern watersheds.

In the 1890s, another part of the story of American forests was taking place in the Blue Ridge Mountains, near Asheville, North Carolina. It began in an unlikely setting, a 250-room mansion modeled on the chateaus of France's Loire Valley—George Washington Vanderbilt's Biltmore. "It would be a suitable and dignified business for you . . . ," the great landscape architect Frederick Law Olmsted told Vanderbilt, ". . . and it would be of great value to the country to have a . . . systematically conducted attempt in forestry made on a large scale."

Olmsted's advice bore fruit. In 1898, a pioneering school of forestry opened on the Vanderbilt estate. And much of the estate's 125,000 acres—some of it run-down farmland—was turned into healthy forest that became the nucleus of the Pisgah, one of the East's first national forests.

Forestry has come a long way from its beginnings on a North Carolina estate. Specialists in different disciplines now work together to fulfill a mandate of assuring a stable supply of water and of timber. "We study plant, soil, and water relationships," said hydrologist Dr. Richard Burns. "Just because you see trees on the slopes as you drive through the

NORTHERN RED OAK
Querus rubra

countryside doesn't automatically mean the watersheds are in good shape," added soil scientist Dan Manning as we sat in the Forest Service office in Asheville.

Richard and Dan were describing the way they determine how a forest area will be affected by activities such as logging or road-building, and how they work to alleviate that impact. "Yet you can't separate the forest from the watershed," Richard continued. "A forest protects the surface of the soil. It maintains good soil conditions so water can go into that soil. No matter what you do to the land you may affect the water, either good or bad."

Dan described a wide diversity of sites, from the deep, rich, well-watered soils of Appalachian coves to the shallow, droughty soils that occur on some steep upper slopes. "Every site is influenced by a variety of interacting factors. Some sites are more easily damaged than others. Once these soils are injured, say by erosion or by compaction by heavy equipment, they take a long time to recover."

"The aim is an even flow of water throughout the year," Richard added. "Think of the land as a big sponge; if you squeeze it, by compacting the soil, or cover it over, you'll have rapid runoff. A watershed in good condition is one that will absorb all rainfall, all snow, and release it all year long."

A badly designed road can be the culprit in damaging a watershed, I learned. These roads are not always logging roads. I drove from valley to valley north of Asheville to Boone, North Carolina. Rainstorms alternated with sunshine and rainbows. Sometimes great slides of mud oozed onto the two-lane highway where condominium builders had gouged steep access roads out of hillsides of native rhododendrons. Recreation is a big business in this region. The Pisgah National Forest, close to the urban East, is home to recreation as much as to timber harvesting. "We are in the people business," one of the rangers told me.

But one spot within the Pisgah—the

breathtaking gorge that drops more than a thousand feet to the Linville River—seems as untouched by people as it must have been on the day in 1766 when hunters William Linville and his son were scalped there by Indians. On a hot, sunny June morning, I joined a Sierra Club group for a hike through Linville Gorge, one of the Pisgah's three wilderness areas. From the west rim, we could see across the gorge to sheer rock walls rising out of unbroken forest that has never been logged. Dark green pines on the high ridges and slopes contrasted with the brighter green of broadleaves. Mountain laurel in pink glory bloomed on the rocky ridges.

Down in the gorge near the river grew stands of hardwoods—tulip trees, sweet gum, maple, oak, and beech. Wildflowers edged the trail and brightened the dark forest floor. Rhododendron thickets crowded near the riverbanks. We camped in a grove of hemlocks near the tumbling river. In the evening, we swam in a deep pool, turned to silver by the full moon.

On another day, though overcast and chilly, it had taken little persuasion to get biologist Ruby Pharr to spend a few hours showing me more of Linville Gorge. We followed a high ridge toward Tablerock Mountain, a promontory on the east side of the gorge. Gnarled pitch and Table Mountain pines clung to the rocky cliffs. Sourwood flowers exuded a heady scent, luring bees that make a type of honey much favored hereabouts.

Ruby teaches at Western Piedmont Community College in Morganton and is something of an expert on wildflowers. She handed me a magnifying eyepiece. Soon I was lost in the heavenly, purple-and-gold center of a spiderwort blossom. "This area is an ideal place to study botany," Ruby said. "With changes in slope exposure, elevation, patches of wet and dry soil, you get a mosaic of species." Our progress was slow, because each plant seemed to have its special lore. We looked

at mushrooms, and mosses, and ferns such as the New York. "You can tell New York fern—it tapers at top and bottom—New Yorkers burn the candle at both ends," Ruby said with a musical laugh. We paused at a chestnut sprouting from an old stump. The sprout represented a futile effort to survive the blight that, in the early part of this century, had wiped out one of the major components of these forests.

"Watch," Ruby said, stooping down quickly to scoop up a millipede in the trail. Bright yellow and black and curling in her hand, it looked for all the world as if its dozens of feet were clad in so many tiny yellow galoshes. "How would you like to buy shoes for him?" Ruby closed her hands around the little creature and shook it up. When she opened her hands, we looked at a rather disoriented millipede, and smelled the scent of almonds. "That's hydrogen cyanide. The millipede secretes it as a defense mechanism."

We leaned out over rock ledges to grab ripe blueberries to eat. The most succulent were, of course, just out of reach down treacherous cliffs. Ruby has probably climbed around these cliffs as much as anyone. One of the rarest plants here is the *Hudsonia montana,* the mountain golden heather. An endemic—a species with a very limited range—the plant grows on these high ridges only on the east side of Linville Gorge. "In order to count them, I had to climb out on the ledges." One time, she told me, she spent a night out here alone under an overhang, just to observe the *Hudsonia*'s brief day of flowering. She showed me a couple of the little plants, past blooming, too insignificant looking to command such devotion.

I saw ample evidence of devotion to these wooded hills in other places I visited. "Plant Trees Grow Jobs," reads a sign on the North Carolina-Tennessee line near Roan Mountain. Many people in this region derive their livelihood from the forests. North Carolina has traditionally ranked as the largest producer of wood furniture in the country. Furniture factories and wood craft shops line rural highways and fringe small towns.

In his workshop near Marion, Max "Pat" Woody makes chairs—sturdy ladderbacks and rockers—out of oak, maple, or walnut. He represents the seventh generation of his family to work in wood. He learned chairmaking from his grandfather. "Possibly people were named by occupation," he said before I'd asked the question. His strong hands turned a chair post on a lathe. He uses no measure. "You gotta go by the feel," he said, peering at me over his glasses. The post, as far as I could see, matched its mates perfectly.

"Wood, that's my livelihood," Paul Pritchard told me at his shop and sawmill outside of Spruce Pine. We were surrounded by slabs of large old walnut, cherry, and maple, some of them probably 400 years old. "Today they cut them too early. In too much of a hurry," Paul said. The tables Paul makes preserve the contour of the tree. They beg for a hand to slide along the silken, swirling grain. "Nature can do more than I can. I just like things natural," he added.

A natural artistry characterized craftsmen I met to the west, in the Great Smoky Mountains. *Shaconage*, "Place of Blue Smoke." So the Smokies were called by the Cherokee Indians who sought game, medicinal plants, and other necessities here long before the white man came. In 1838 most of the tribe was forced to march westward on the Trail of Tears, relocated to the territory that became Oklahoma. More than a thousand Cherokees avoided that tragic march by taking refuge in these rugged mountains, surviving on roots and small animals. Some four thousand died on that journey. "It was too sad," said Martha Ross. "Most of our race was wiped out."

Descendants of those fugitives form the Eastern Band of the Cherokee. I met Martha and her friend Carol Welch, members of the Eastern Band, at Cherokee, North Carolina. Both women are basketmakers. In Carol's kitchen, where she works, I watched strong, nimble hands pull long strips of dyed split oak in and out. Gradually an intricate design emerged in an urn-shaped basket. "Black comes from butternut, brown from walnut. The red I get from bloodroot." Carol uses young white oaks cut deep in the forest and peeled into thin splits. "I make about a dozen baskets a week, all different sizes. It's tiring work," she said. "But I'd be lost if I didn't have it to do."

The Smokies, among the highest mountains in the East, include a large remnant of the vast virgin forest that once covered eastern North America. About 35 percent of the half-million-acre Great Smoky Mountains National Park is old-growth forest. In the late 1970s the park was designated an International Biosphere Reserve by UNESCO, cited as "perhaps the best example of undisturbed hardwood forest in the United States." It is an area of recognized diversity, with 1,500 species of vascular plants, including more than a hundred kinds of trees—more than in all of northern Europe.

Long ago, the region was the repository of many species that died out farther north. "During the Ice Age, the glaciers never reached this far south though the climate was very much colder. Plant zones here were displaced to lower elevations but not wiped out," said Dr. Peter S. White, botanist at the Uplands Field Research Laboratory in the park. We chatted at his home, where he lives with his wife, Carolyn, their daughter, Sarah, and a fluffy cat named Linnaeus—after the great Swedish botanist.

"Europe is a pauper in species diversity compared with this area," the young botanist explained. "Part of the reason lies in the way major mountain ranges are aligned. In North America, the mountains run generally north-south. But in Europe they go east-west, thus presenting a formidable barrier for the plants that were retreating from the increasing cold."

I learned more about the Smokies'

botanical history from Dr. Aaron J. Sharp. Botany professor emeritus at the University of Tennessee in Knoxville, Dr. Sharp can out-hike people half his age. He was planning a climb up Mount Le Conte to celebrate his 80th birthday. This day he invited me to join him on an easy walk toward Porters Flat in the Greenbrier Cove area, one of the finest cove hardwood sites in the park.

"I believe these mountains have been here, available for plant occupancy, as long as there have been flowering plants," Dr. Sharp said. Some scientists think the primitive flowering plants included the magnolia family, still prominent here. Dr. Sharp continued: "There can be a lot of mutations even in 70 or 80 million years. With the variety of environments here, a lot of new species could survive."

Dr. Sharp showed me some of the scores of trees and smaller plants that make up a complex hardwood community. We rested on an old log that was a garden of mosses, ferns, and seedlings. Dr. Sharp has remained a student of the Smokies for 55 years. Mosses are his speciality, but his interests are not limited. Hospitals call on him in plant poisonings. Once two men fell deathly ill after eating what they believed were ramps. "I thought of false hellebore or bead lily. False hellebore has been known to kill a cow. The men recovered. It turned out they had eaten ramps, as well as false hellebore."

Professor Sharp has tried to impart his encompassing view of plants to his students. "The problem is to make students realize their total dependence on photosynthesis. Name a textile, name a food that doesn't ultimately come from plants. With a better understanding of the plant world, people have a better understanding of their place in the universe."

I had missed spring in the Smokies, that burst of trilliums, violets, irises, lady's slippers, and spring beauties that seize the narrow window of light and warmth that comes before the trees leaf out. Still, as I walked up Ramsay Cascades in the

AMERICAN BEECH
Fagus grandifolia

Greenbrier Cove area one morning, I was greeted by bluets, wood sorrel, bead lily, foam flower, galax—and my favorite, the tiny, white-flowered partridgeberry.

As I climbed higher, the trees were older and larger—tulip trees, maples, buckeyes, hemlocks that no ax had ever threatened. This was late June, the time some mountain people call the "dark season," when the canopy of leaves closes out all but marginal light. Polypody, maidenhair, Christmas, silver, and rattlesnake ferns sprouted from rocks and rotting logs. Rhododendrons clung to the edge of clear, rushing Ramsay Prong. The air exuded a fresh, rich, earthy scent.

At the falls I could see slender strands of water streaming a hundred feet down a rock face. Great purple globes of catawba rhododendrons bloomed at the very top of the falls. I recalled what park ranger Glenn Cardwell had said of this area, where he grew up. "God made Greenbrier first," Glenn told me. "He did such a good job, He decided to make heaven!"

In a remote upland corner of northern Alabama, south and west of the Great Smokies, the Cumberland Plateau meets the upper coastal plain. Rivers here have carved gorges where hardwood forests thrive akin to those of mountains farther north. Settlers came here in the early 19th century. The land reminded them of the hills they'd left in Georgia and North Carolina. An independent lot, they subsisted on a corn patch, a garden, a little cotton, and the game from the forest. These people were no slave owners. During the Civil War they just wanted to be left alone. Many refused to join either side and hid out in the woods, supported by the local citizenry. This determined neutrality earned the area the nickname of the "Free State of Winston."

I drove across rolling hills toward the 12,726-acre Sipsey Wilderness, in the Bankhead National Forest. Chicken farms and Freewill Baptist churches line the roads here. Logging trucks labor up the long grades to small mills. At the Sipsey, I met Helen Kittinger and John Findlay III, both members of the Audubon Society and bird-watchers avid enough to drive a thousand miles to Michigan to see a Kirtland's warbler. Helen was long involved in the protection of the Sipsey, which in 1975 became one of the East's first designated wildernesses. "They were clear-cutting large areas before then, just destroying our forests," Helen said.

Helen sees a continuing threat to Alabama's upland hardwood forests—conversion. That is the term foresters use for the management practice of transforming a woodland from one type of timber to another. Forestry is Alabama's major industry. A large portion of the logging takes place farther south, in the pine areas. But even in the north, the trend among some loggers has been to favor fast-growing, marketable pines over hardwoods. To give the less competitive loblolly pines a chance in this area, after loggers clearcut, foresters must use herbicides to knock back the native hardwoods. And with the shorter harvest cycle for the pines, the hardwoods that do survive never reach mature size.

"This just wasn't intended to be a pine area," added Helen emphatically, her brown eyes flashing behind large glasses. "That wasn't what God had in mind when He planted it." It is such practices as conversion that make protected pockets of native hardwood like the Sipsey even more precious. Near the northern boundary of the wilderness area, we walked among wild geraniums, wood betony, daisy-like coreopis, and sweet ciceley. Helen made soft *pish-pish* sounds to coax the birds closer. An indigo bunting answered cheerily, then a black-throated green warbler. The warbler nests here in the Eastern hemlocks, Helen said. Like many of the forests I had visited, the Sipsey is a mixture of northern and southern flora. "In some areas of the Sipsey in fall you'd think you were in New England —with the color of the sugar maples, sweet gums, oaks, and tulip trees."

Early on another day, I headed out to canoe the Sipsey Wilderness with district ranger Jim Hughes and two of the Forest Service staff, Richard Evans and Ted Freeman. Birders, hikers, hunters, and wild animals must share the Sipsey. But in spring, when the water is up, it belongs mostly to the paddlers. Soon we were gliding on the green waters of Thompson Creek, a tributary of the Sipsey Fork. Dick and I shared one canoe, Jim and Ted the other. Tulip trees reached a hundred feet above us, interspersed with maples, beeches, and sycamores. Rivulets burbled down to the creek from both sides. Boulders and bluffs rose shadowy behind a veil of green. As long as 8,000 years ago, Indians lived in the area under weathered sandstone overhangs.

Honeysuckle in full bloom scented the air. A blue-and-black butterfly wafted across the bow of the canoe. But our idyllic cruise was soon rudely interrupted. A large tree downed across the creek turned out to be only the first of many logjams. Sometimes we could slide the canoes beneath. Other times we had to climb onto the logs and drag the boats over the top. Once we hauled the canoes out of the water and portaged for a hundred yards or so.

Near where Thompson and Hubbard Creeks join to form the Sipsey Fork, we stopped above the one real rapid we would face, a sinuous S-curve where the water squeezes between large boulders. Ted and Dick decided to try it in one canoe. Jim and I opted for a short portage. For a minute we thought Ted and Dick had made it. Then the canoe smacked into a rock, turned over, and dumped the two men into the foaming water. Jim and I were feeling pretty smug and dry onshore—until we remembered that all the food was in that canoe, fast heading downstream upside down. We caught the boat. Lunch was only a little soggy.

Long shadows stretched across the river by the time we pulled ashore, weary but enchanted by the Sipsey's special

world. Later, I went back into the wilderness area for one last visit. I camped in a grove of trees near Bee Branch, one of the creeks that feed the Sipsey Fork. In the morning I stood somewhat in awe before the Big Tree, the biggest tulip tree in Alabama, with a girth of 20 feet, 8 inches.

Behind the tree, over the rim of the box canyon that has protected it for all its long life, poured two 50-foot waterfalls. Morning sun crept gradually into the gorge, catching the pale green spring leaves atop the 151-foot giant. Other large trees grew in the little cove, but at a distance, like nobles in respectful attendance to a monarch.

From the Sipsey, I headed to Arkansas and the Ozarks, near the western edge of the eastern deciduous forest. Though the Ozarks share many of the characteristics of eastern woodlands, you would never mistake these flat-topped mountains, rarely higher than 2,500 feet and generally level with each other, for the imposing peaks of the Smokies and the Blue Ridge. The Ozark highlands once lay beneath a vast sea. Sediments formed layers of limestone and sandstone, and the region was gradually uplifted. Then water, cutting ever deeper, shaped the rugged canyons and gorges of today.

From high ridges north of Russellville, I could look into these slashes in the land, which appeared as thickly forested as they must have been when naturalist Thomas Nuttall traveled in the region in 1819. Nuttall described "One vast trackless wilderness of trees . . . still preserving its primeval type, its unreclaimed exuberance." However, like the East, the Ozarks did not escape destructive farming practices and rapacious timber operations. A portion of these depleted lands has been protected and restored in Arkansas' Ozark National Forest, established in 1908 by Teddy Roosevelt. A few other areas in the forest escaped devastation by their very remoteness.

Flowing northward in the Boston Mountains to meet the Buffalo River,

YELLOW BUCKEYE
Aesculus octandra

Richland Creek carves a rugged little gorge that still seems untouched. For me, the Richland Creek area quickly became a kaleidoscope: of men chatting in a general store; of a tight-lipped old moonshiner; of friendly waves from passing pickup trucks; of a gnarled old woman plowing her garden behind a mule; of peckerwood mills, small sawmills in the forest; of a ginseng or "sang" digger and his lore; and of the eyes of an old man lighting up at the thought of a feast of baked coon and spring greens from the woods. "It's the kind of place," said Chip Ernst, forester in the Buffalo District, "where people talk five minutes on a wrong number."

With Chip and Kathy Waters, also of the Forest Service staff, I set out early one morning for a hike to Richland Falls. Chip mentioned that in the old days, moonshiners hid out in these woods. Soon we were bushwhacking across a steep slope, thick with second-growth hickories and oaks. We dropped toward the boulder-choked creek in spring spate. Huge sweet gums and sycamores leaned out from Richland's bank. "Only crazy people canoe this," Chip said.

The trail, I thought, wasn't much easier. It was simple to understand how the Richland gorge has remained so wild. We inched along, climbing up and down slippery slopes and across crumbling sandstone bluffs and ledges. Many times Chip gallantly hauled Kathy and me up steep places or steadied us down slippery stretches. It started to rain heavily. "How much farther?" Kathy and I would ask. "About half a mile," Chip would reply. That was the answer we got for the next two hours. But the falls were worth it. They extend a hundred feet across the entire creek, spilling into a deep, blue-green pool that lured us for a soothing swim.

Throughout these woodlands, the predominant trees are oak and hickory. In a way, Charles Christian's chairs tell a tale of the Ozark forests. I met the chairmaker at his workshop near Mount Judea, Arkansas. He lives on land his great-grandfather homesteaded. For the last 20 years, Charles and his family have made ladderbacks, rockers, and stools out of stout oak and hickory.

"I can pick out my chairs," Charles says—with justifiable pride, I thought, as I looked at a set of six graceful ladderbacks he had recently finished. "Everyone turns just a little bit different on the lathe." Charles combines chairmaking with duties as pastor of a local church and numerous other interests. A tall, redheaded man with a soft drawl, he told me about his craft. He explained how the posts of the chairs are left green, but the rungs are dried—in the kitchen stove for 72 hours at low heat. That way the green posts will shrink as they dry and grip the rungs tightly. No glue is needed.

Outside, in back of the shop, Charles prepares bitternut hickory for the woven seats. He showed me how he uses a drawknife to remove the rough outer bark then swiftly peel strips of the inner bark. "In summer the strips come loose more easily," he said, "but in winter you get better bark—it doesn't shrink up on you."

Charles cuts the hickory in the Ozark National Forest. A few years ago herbicides and aerial spraying caused quite a controversy in this forest. In some areas, hardwoods such as bitternut hickory were being killed. Conversion to pine was the goal. After a court injunction and a long period of litigation, the national forest abandoned aerial spraying, agreeing to apply chemicals by hand and to use them only in specific situations.

The stricter controls mean added protection for the forest's understory as well as for its trees. "Some of my best friends are plants," said Gary Tucker. *Phacelia ranunculacea, Asclepias quadrifolia, Delphinium newtonianum* . . . the sonorous Latin phrases flowed. But for the jeans instead of a toga, Gary might have been discussing the fair ladies of ancient Rome instead of conferring with his colleague on the flowering beauties of the Ozarks.

I had joined Dr. Tucker, Professor of Botany at Arkansas Tech University in Russellville and a member of the Arkansas Natural Heritage Commission, and Steve Orzell, botanist with the commission. The two men were looking for rare plants in the national forest. Though they used the Latin nomenclature universal in the field, they were kind enough to give the common names also as they pointed out trees and flowers.

"A large portion of what we see here is also found in the East," said Gary. Like the southern Appalachians, the Ozarks were never glaciated during the Ice Age, and they too offered a biological haven. "Though the Ozarks are drier and don't have all the variety of the East, there still is tremendous variety in micro-pockets of plant communities."

Steve and Gary's major worry is that certain logging practices and other activities in the forest will damage or even wipe out rare plants. "You need to get out and show people what plants there are," Gary remarked. "Otherwise, they say 'Big deal—woods is woods . . . second growth is as good as first.' But in clear-cutting, for instance, all the shade-loving plants go right away." Added Steve, "Most people don't realize, if they just drive through the Ozarks, that this isn't just a bunch of rocks and oaks. We have marvelous glades with southwestern flora, upland ponds harboring coastal species, and deep hollows with glacial relicts—plants that have survived here even after the Ice Age."

I felt fortunate to meet a few of Gary Tucker's "friends" in the Ozarks. Before I left, Gary and his wife, Sharon, gave me one to take home. A cluster of bright red flowers poked from the top of a big box. "*Spigelia marilandica*, Indian Pink," Gary said. "It likes shade and acid soil." With a little luck I shall have this friend blooming in my yard each spring to remind me of the forest communities I had visited, and of the many people who showed me that rich and complex world.

*P*owerful Shay locomotive gathers steam for an excursion in the mountainous terrain of eastern West Virginia. The Cass Scenic Railroad follows an old logging route through wooded Appalachian hillsides. Many forests of the southeastern highlands nearly succumbed to logging around the turn of the century, when railroads opened the steepest, most remote gorges to timber cutters. Fires sometimes followed. On Black Mountain, southwest of the town of Cass, biologist Ed Buck sits on rocks exposed by a devastating fire he witnessed in the 1930s. "All the vegetation was completely consumed," he says, "the plant loam of thousands of years."

PRECEDING PAGES: *Fisherman casts for trout in the Cranberry River on a hazy morning. To the east lies the Cranberry Wilderness, a 35,864-acre portion of the Monongahela National Forest.*

TIM THOMPSON

EDWARD SCHELL (ABOVE AND LEFT)

*B*lue beeches shade riffling waters of the Middle Prong of the Little Pigeon River in Great Smoky Mountains National Park. The 520,000-acre sanctuary in Tennessee and North Carolina shelters hundreds of varieties of trees and smaller plants, each finding its own environmental niche. At left, round-leaved yellow violets snatch spring's light before trees leaf out. Shade-tolerant partridgeberries (far left) flower even in summer. The brightly colored berries remain from the previous season.

Mother black bear and cub retreat to a leafy refuge high in a tulip tree in the Smokies. The park's rugged recesses shelter more than 400 black bears as well as many other kinds of wildlife. Protected within the park from human threat, the bears face a new danger—the European wild boar. The prolific hogs, introduced to the area by hunters in 1912, now number more than a thousand. The boars devour nuts and berries, foods favored by black bears. Their aggressive rooting may also endanger many forest plants.

FOLLOWING PAGES: *Catawba rhododendrons blush atop Roan Mountain along the Tennessee-North Carolina border. Such openings in the forest—called balds— have long intrigued botanists studying the southern Appalachians.*

"*I* *started wood as a rainy day job,*" *says Edd Presnell. In his workshop near Banner Elk,*
North Carolina, Presnell cradles a dulcimer he fashioned of curly maple, chestnut, and walnut.
He also crafts utilitarian objects, from bowls to caskets—in keeping with a regional tradition
of "make, make-do, or do without." In sharp contrast to such frugality, the 250-room mansion
Biltmore (above) rises near Asheville. In the 1890s, George Washington Vanderbilt spared
no expense in its construction. Vanderbilt also spared no effort in his dedication to America's
woodlands: The nation's first practical school of forestry began on his estate in 1898.

*T*enacious roots push through a
moss-covered boulder (right) in
northwestern Alabama's Sipsey
Wilderness area, part of the
Bankhead National Forest.
Resembling green hair atop a
gnarled visage, resurrection fern
and moss sprout on a weathered
log (left). Below, shriveled beech
leaves swirl over the shattered
gravestone of a young woman
who died here during another
autumn long ago. A pine seedling
emerges through a crack in
the gravestone, symbolic of the
forest's endless cycle of life.

"*There is no place,*" *observed naturalist John Muir, "so impressively solitary as a dense forest with a stream passing over a rocky bed." On its way to the West Sipsey Fork, Turkey Creek cascades down sandstone ledges. This tranquil haven lies within the 12,726-acre Sipsey Wilderness. Countless streams lace the slopes of the southeastern highlands; Ice Age glaciers, which elsewhere gouged out lakes and ponds, never reached this far south.*

*L*ichen-splattered boulders overlook forested ridges near Richland Creek in the Ozarks of northern Arkansas (left). The Ozarks preserve a wealth of complex plant communities. Here, scrubby pines and cedars, along with coppery-colored low-bush huckleberries, survive on thin soils. The nectar of ironweed draws a great spangled fritillary butterfly (above). Below, a carpenter bee lands on a passionflower, and luminous mushrooms sprout from a rotting log. Fungi play a vital role in the forest, helping break down dead plant and animal matter to form new soil.

TIM ERNST

Ghostly relic molders amid the profuse growth of an Ozark woodland. A hardwood sapling shoots up through the old automobile's engine compartment as the forest reclaims its domain. The Ozarks—moderately watered and mild of climate—show resilience in recovering from past abuses. Near the western edge of the eastern deciduous forest, the Ozarks form a sort of botanical crossroads, where plants from north, south, east, and west meet. "Leaflet three, let it be," goes an adage about poison ivy (below, left). Young vines climb beside a thick old vine on a black gum tree.

W*ith the pride of a skilled craftsman, Charles Christian puts finishing touches on a ladderback chair in his shop near Mount Judea, Arkansas. At left he weaves the last strips of bitternut hickory inner bark into the seat. "The bark is moist, right from the tree. When it dries it's very rugged." The Ozark chairmaker uses green wood for posts and seasoned wood for rungs. The posts shrink as they dry, taking a vise-like grip on the rungs. "The chair has no nails or glue in it," he points out. Choosing the right piece of wood calls on skills gained over a lifetime. "I've learned to see deep into the wood," says Christian.*

The Southern Cornucopia

By H. Robert Morrison
Photographs by Tim Thompson

LOBLOLLY PINE
Pinus taeda

NOSE TO NOSE, only their eyes breaking the still surface of the swamp, the alligators regarded each other. For a full minute they held motionless—the six-foot mother facing the smaller alligator that had swum into the territory where she guarded her foot-long babies. Without a ripple the mother sank beneath the surface. All remained calm, the stillness broken only by the cry of songbirds and the occasional boom of a bullfrog.

Suddenly mama lunged. Thrashing tails shattered the stillness; a thwack shivered the boardwalk where I stood. I waited, expecting to see reptilian blood staining the water and mama emerging with a mouthful of alligator. But again, all was still. Several minutes passed before I glimpsed the smaller animal swimming away—chastened but uninjured as far as I could tell. When mama surfaced among the green clumps of water lettuce floating at the far edge of the pool, she briefly inspected one of her young, then submerged again.

This scene unfolded at the National Audubon Society's Corkscrew Swamp Sanctuary, northwest of Everglades National Park. Corkscrew Swamp Sanctuary is home to a profusion of plant and animal species—an abundance typical of the woodlands that I visited along the coastal plain. The forests of this region fall into three broad categories: lowland and floodplain prairies and swamps, characterized by bald cypress and tupelo along with a few other varieties tolerant of prolonged flooding; drier upland woods, consisting of sandy hilltops and plateaus that are home to pines; and between these extremes, hardwood forests and mixed stands of broadleafs and conifers.

For a glimpse of the few remaining virgin stands of these forest types, I explored Corkscrew Swamp Sanctuary and nearby Big Cypress National Preserve; Congaree Swamp National Monument southeast of Columbia, South Carolina; and Big Thicket National Preserve headquartered at Beaumont, Texas. Finally, at Noxubee National Wildlife Refuge south of Starkville, Mississippi, I learned how sound forestry practices can contribute to the improvement of woodland-wildlife habitats.

My travels began at Big Cypress National Preserve. Driving west from Miami on the Tamiami Trail, U. S. Highway 41, toward the preserve's headquarters at Ochopee, I peered at saw grass flats and prairie land stretching into the distance, punctuated by clumps of trees. My first reaction was to wonder just where the forests were.

At Big Cypress Preserve, I discovered one explanation for the random groups of trees: A vast sheet of water, inches deep but miles wide, covers this area, funneling rainwater from southwestern Florida toward Everglades National Park. Here, in most places, mere inches of soil cover the limestone of the Florida plain, offering little foothold for trees. In places, however, shallow depressions in the limestone hold deeper pockets of soil where trees can take root.

"Even a few inches of difference in either soil or water depth can mean an entirely different plant community," Bruce Freet told me. The managing biologist for Big Cypress Preserve, Bruce is a compact, muscular man with a thick, neatly trimmed brown beard. At the edge of a stand of cypress—called a dome for its rounded shape—Bruce showed me what he meant. We stood ankle-deep in water; all about the dome stretched a prairie where occasional cabbage palmettos raised fanlike fronds and scattered grasses grew in clusters.

Willows fringed the dome, their gray-green leaves fluttering listlessly in a faint breeze. As we waded farther into the deepening depression, the water rose above our ankles. Here stood small pond cypresses, considered a variety of bald cypress by some botanists and a distinct species by others. A hundred yards or so farther, having carefully avoided clumps of saw grass—"Prime habitat for cottonmouths," Bruce warned—we reached the open center of the dome.

"Large pond cypresses grow around the depression where soil and water conditions are ideal," Bruce explained. "But the deep water in the center of the dome restricts cypress regeneration. That's one reason why you get this 'hole in the doughnut' appearance."

Domes are not the only places where cypresses flourish in the preserve. The sheet of water inching toward Everglades National Park has worn several shallow channels here, and in these grow long stretches of cypress, called strands. Most strands now contain smaller, second-growth trees, for the demand for rot-resistant cypress wood drew lumber companies to the region beginning in the 1930s. One area that escaped the saw is Big Cypress Bend, a portion of the Fakahatchee Strand State Preserve just west of Big Cypress National Preserve.

Designated a national natural land-mark in 1966, Big Cypress Bend appears today much as it did when Columbus made landfall in the New World. The Florida Department of Natural Resources has built a boardwalk into the heart of the strand, where visitors can see the incredible diversity of life in this fecund forest.

In the shade of hundred-foot-tall bald cypresses grow palmettos, their yard-wide fronds spotlighted by shafts of sunlight piercing the dense canopy. Reaching above the understory like giant umbrellas, green fronds of the rare Florida royal palm sprout atop smooth trunks the color of newly poured concrete. The soft, persistent hum of mosquitoes and the rustle of occasional falling leaves accompany the tangy, pervasive odor of rotting vegetation.

Here plants thrive wherever there is a foot of open ground; when that doesn't exist, they find somewhere else to grow. Ferns spring from fallen trunks of trees—the giant leather fern sometimes growing ten feet tall. Resurrection ferns cling to branches, curled tight and brown. A brief shower brings them once again to life, open and green.

About halfway along its 2,000-foot length, the walkway divides around a giant bald cypress whose trunk stands entwined by a sinuous network of wrist-thick roots. Untold years ago the sticky seed of a strangler fig settled onto a branch of the tree, sprouted, and sent its roots down more than a hundred feet to the moist forest floor. As the invading plant flourished, its roots circled the tree in an enveloping grip—one that could have killed a smaller tree.

The boardwalk ends at the edge of an open pond deep within the strand. There I leaned against the railing and marveled at how this abundance of plant life is mirrored in the richness of animal life. As I watched, a five-foot alligator probed pickerelweeds and arrowhead plants growing in shallow water near the edge of the pond. Two black vultures settled on the chalky limbs of a dead cypress at the far side. Half a dozen young cotton-mouths, about six inches long, sunned on a protruding tree root a few feet away, occasionally slipping into the water and stalking small fish.

A hoarse scream off to the right startled me. Through my binoculars, I caught a glimpse of a dark snake holding a large green bullfrog in its mouth as it slithered over a fallen tree trunk. Another cry from the frog, then stillness settled again. If I could observe so many wild creatures in such a short time, I thought to myself, how many more must live unseen in this watery world?

Within the Big Cypress Preserve, water is just one of the factors that shape the environment. "Fire's just as important as water," Bruce Freet had told me, and today he was showing me why. We had trailered three-wheel all-terrain cycles—giant motorized tricycles with knobbed balloon tires—to an oil rig where Bruce parked. Because of its status as a preserve, drilling is allowed here. The Park Service and other agencies, however, maintain strict environmental safeguards.

We mounted the cycles and drove northwest of the drilling rig. Bruce told me he had set a prescribed, or supervised, burn here, and the results at first glance looked horrible. The earth lay blackened, a scorched contrast to the lush green grass across the dirt track that had served as a firebreak.

When I mentioned how barren it appeared, Bruce smiled. "We burned this just last week," he said. "It's been a year since we fired that other patch, and you couldn't tell it was ever burned without looking closely. But there are already signs of recovery here." He nudged a green shoot of grass with the toe of his boot and reached in his pocket for a tape measure. "Let's see just how well this is doing." I was surprised by what I saw when he held the rule against the grass: In a single week, a green blade fully four inches long had developed.

"For centuries," Bruce said, "the Big Cypress, especially in pine and grass areas like this, caught fire from lightning. To thrive, plants had to survive occasional burning. Then man began suppressing fires, and we found that the environment was changing. Hardwoods and shrubs not resistant to fire were taking over. Dead grasses and branches were accumulating. When fires began, they quickly grew so hot even fire-tolerant plants died.

"That's why we're using prescribed fires regularly now. The burning maintains the natural selection of plant communities. It prevents fuel buildup and thus keeps accidental fires more manageable. And it quickly returns nutrients to the soil."

Leaving Big Cypress National Preserve, I drove northwest to Corkscrew Swamp Sanctuary, the site of major rookeries for the endangered wood stork, the only stork native to the United States. Corkscrew was established as a sanctuary by the National Audubon Society in 1954, with the help of contributions from individuals and from two local businesses, Lee Tidewater Cypress Company and Collier Enterprises. Corkscrew is one of the finest cypress swamps in the world. Here grow bald cypress trees 140 feet tall and more than 500 years old.

When I visited Corkscrew, the wood storks' young had already hatched. "You can hear them, and if you watch patiently, you might see a downy head peeking over the nest," chief naturalist Rick Bantz told me in the visitor center. I set off down the long boardwalk that opens Corkscrew Swamp to visitors.

Crossing a wet prairie, the walkway led to the fringe of the cypress forest where smaller pond cypresses grew. In southern Florida, pond cypresses grow in drier locations and on thinner topsoil than bald cypresses. These trees have foliage that grows with overlapping scales and looks very different from the feathery tops of the giant bald cypress. Both cypresses, however, share an unusual characteristic: In winter, unlike most conifers, the trees lose their needles.

Farther along, such water-tolerant trees as red maples and pop ash rose from the water. In their shade, wax myrtle, ferns, and custard apple trees grew along with dahoon holly, a relative of the decorative Christmas greenery. Tiny disks of floating fern spotted open patches of water, in some places blanketing the surface with green.

I could hear the cheeping of the young wood storks before I saw their nests, piles of sticks high up in the cypresses. Mature birds perched like daubs of white paint among the branches, their dark, unfeathered heads almost comically ugly. With a noisy flapping, an adult would take flight, revealing the black trailing edges of its wings, which span some five feet. As I watched them, I was fascinated by the fact that these large birds could perch on such thin branches.

I saw one wood stork land near a nest with a furious, ungainly backpedaling of wings. Looking through my binoculars, I could just see a downy white head. The parent fed the chick, then edged back as its mate landed with another morsel. Some 1,200 wood storks fledged successfully at Corkscrew in 1984, Rick Bantz told me. That was a good year, especially considering the high springtime water levels that made food-gathering difficult for parent birds.

Rick cares deeply about the fate of the wood stork. "If we can ensure the stork's future here in southern Florida," he said, "we're going to ensure a better quality of life for other wildlife, as well as for ourselves.

"South Florida has been a tropical paradise, but man has been changing the environment here for many years. Birds have been called the litmus paper of our natural environment, and that's true. The decline of the wood stork should have been like bells going off, warning us that something was wrong."

SWEET GUM
Liquidambar styraciflua

Florida's Corkscrew Sanctuary and Big Cypress Preserve certainly impressed me with their variety of plant life, but when I visited Big Thicket National Preserve north of Beaumont, Texas, I found the range of forest types astonishing. The Big Thicket is a biological crossroads, where the southern swamplands meet the eastern hardwood forests and the desert vegetation of the Southwest. Here location, geology, and climate have combined to produce an amazing botanical diversity.

Although they never reached this far south, glaciers helped shape the Big Thicket. During warmer periods between four major Ice Age glaciations, meltwater from the receding ice refilled the Gulf of Mexico. As sea level rose, streams carrying the overflow deposited sediments along the shoreline, creating deltas, and eventually alluvial plains. The result was the formation of a basin that gently slopes toward the Gulf, an area today containing soils ranging from clay to loam to sand.

Climate has continued to affect the Big Thicket. Mild winters average in the mid-50s and summers in the mid-80s; the four seasons remain distinct, yet wildflowers bloom year-round. The area receives abundant rainfall, averaging between 50 and 60 inches a year.

These conditions combined to produce a truly Big Thicket—a region of tangled jungle and open, parklike stands of towering longleaf pines; cypress swamps and impenetrable canebrakes; savanna wetlands where longleaf and shortleaf pines tower above blueberries and native orchids; and deserts with prickly pear and yucca growing a few yards from a mixed forest of oaks, beeches, magnolias, and loblolly pines. Here, too, are baygalls—acid swamps named for their combination of sweet bay and gallberry holly—and river floodplains where giant palmettos stand thick in the shade of overcup oaks, willow oaks, and other water-tolerant hardwoods.

In the 19th century, a handful of

settlers carved out a self-sufficient pioneer existence on the fringes of this wild expanse; a sprinkling of the disaffected—including outlaws and men who declined to be drafted into Civil War armies—vanished into its interior. The Big Thicket waited, little changed, until around the turn of the century. Then lumber companies discovered its trees; railroads cut through its wilderness; and in 1901, the Spindletop field near Beaumont set off the first Texas oil rush.

"You can't see any of the real Big Thicket from the highway," plant ecologist Geraldine Watson told me. "It's all changed—overrun by farms and housing developments, by towns and timber plantations." Of the Big Thicket's estimated original three and a half million acres, only a fraction remains unaltered. In 1974, after years of conflict between conservationists and logging interests, Congress set aside 84,550 acres. The preserve was intended to protect representative remnants of each of the Big Thicket's plant communities, and includes several of its least disturbed portions.

To me, the Big Thicket National Preserve is a park that almost isn't there. It consists of a dozen areas, most of them unmarked, scattered along dusty back roads and river bottoms north and west of Beaumont. Visitors who don't have a guide and don't know the local landmarks have difficulty finding many of the preserve's units.

"Congress hasn't authorized one cent for development since the preserve was established," Superintendent Thomas E. Lubbert explained. "So far, with volunteer help and a few dollars from our maintenance budget, we've been able to open a small visitor center and build a few trails; that's about all."

Geraldine Watson, a wiry woman with wavy silver hair and a determined jut of the jaw, has spent her life in and for the Big Thicket. As much as anyone, she was responsible for the establishment of the preserve. An accomplished botanist, she works for the National Park Service, inventorying the preserve's 85 species of trees and its more than one thousand kinds of flowering plants.

With Geraldine, I explored a savanna west of Hickory Creek. Here prairie grasses grew knee-high on the sandy soil. Towers of mud pellets stood above holes where crayfish had burrowed down to the damp subsoil. Club mosses, plants whose ancient relatives once grew as tall as trees, sprouted green stems as big around as my little finger.

As we strolled toward a stand of longleaf pines, Geraldine didn't like what she saw. Among the pines were small dogwoods and other deciduous trees. "This should be much more open under the pines," she remarked. "It will take three or four fires to reestablish this upland pine community the way it used to be.

"Fire was what gave the Big Thicket so much of its diversity," she continued. "These uplands once burned during regular cycles of drought. The fires killed deciduous trees, loblolly pines, and other species that couldn't tolerate the burning. The forests thus never reached the climax stage; instead, they remained in a perpetual subclimax stage."

One evening as Geraldine and I drove back to Beaumont after a day in the woods, I asked her what it was like growing up in the Big Thicket. "The thing I remember most is the sound of the wind in the longleaf pines," she said. "There never was such sweet music as that."

I heard some of Big Thicket's music in the Neches Bottom and Jack Gore Baygall Unit, which threads along the floodplain of the Neches River. With chief naturalist David Dunatchik, I hiked through a forest of mixed pines and hardwoods, pausing to admire the purple and green jack-in-the-pulpits hiding close to the ground under their wide leaves. As we walked along a gentle hillside, the landscape changed abruptly. Even the sound of our footsteps signaled a difference.

Before, we had crunched over dry, fallen leaves; now we squished through black, boot-tugging muck. We had entered a baygall. Rather than draining away, the water here stood hardly moving. Trees still towered above us, but instead of loblollys and beeches, there were sweet bay magnolias and several other water-tolerant species. We clambered onto the exposed roots of a giant swamp chestnut oak and looked around.

"Because water accumulates here, it leaches tannin from the fallen leaves," said David. "That's what gives the water its dark color, like strong tea, and makes it very acid. Some plants can't live under these conditions, but many others thrive here."

David began identifying the plants around us. Netted chain and Christmas ferns grew amid clumps of sphagnum moss. Greenbrier, poison ivy, rattan, and muscadine grape vines hung from the branches of American holly and gallberry holly. Shrubby trees called titi formed a dense thicket that shaded a patch of jack-in-the-pulpits. In all, we counted 19 different plant species within a dozen feet.

Big Thicket claims four of the five types of carnivorous plants found in the United States: the bladderwort and butterwort, the tiny sundew, and the towering pitcher plant. Only the Venus flytrap is missing. Near the eastern boundary of the preserve's Turkey Creek Unit I came upon several acres of pitcher plants, their tubular leaves tapering a foot or more to the base. Peering inside one, I saw the half-digested remains of insects that had crawled into the plant and become trapped there by downward-pointing hairs.

Though the pitcher plants were fascinating, it was not the unusual plants such as these that I found most interesting in the Big Thicket. Most intriguing to me was the way ordinary trees and plants lived in unusual combinations—eastern forest species growing with typically southern pines; prairie grasses flourishing within sight of eastern dogwoods; and dense, damp titi thickets rising a few yards from prickly pear cactus plants. It was as if nature had decided to grow her own arboretum here in eastern Texas.

I found a far different setting from the Big Thicket area southeast of Columbia, South Carolina. There I explored Congaree Swamp National Monument, a remnant of the bottomland hardwood forests that once extended along floodplains throughout the Southeast.

When I first visited the monument, in early May 1984, the Congaree River was flooding. That's not unusual; it happens an average of ten times a year. Like most of the rivers in South Carolina, the Congaree remains unchanneled, free to overflow its banks.

Most of the monument lay underwater. When park naturalist Fran Rametta offered to guide me on a walk through the flooded forest, I accepted immediately. We set out on the road that leads into the swamp. A few hundred yards from the ranger station, the gentle downhill slope of the road disappeared under a sheet of water. Following the submerged road around a curve, we came to an area where laurel oaks and giant loblolly pines grew. Averaging about 135 feet tall, the pines cast shimmering reflections on the smooth surface of the dark water.

We could hear birds all around us—warblers, cardinals, the hammering tattoo of the pileated woodpecker—but except for an occasional glimpse, they remained invisible. Beyond the road's edge, where thick patches of honeysuckle and other plants formed a dense border, the water stretched as far as we could see. Half-submerged branches and taller weedy plants bobbed in the current like tethered kites straining to break free.

The water had nearly reached our knees when Fran pointed out a change in its color. We could see distinctly where the pale gray, silt-laden water of the Congaree flowed through the clear, tea-colored water of Cedar Creek before they intermingled. "One reason the trees grow so big here," Fran said, "is because of the fertile silt regularly deposited by floods. That helps explain why we've had a number of state and national champion trees—the largest recorded examples of their species. Also, much of the monument was never logged; these trees have had time to grow.

"Sometimes it's hard to realize how big these trees are, because their neighbors are big, too. And there's nothing of normal scale to compare them to. When I applied for this job, another ranger I knew who had visited Congaree Swamp kidded me. 'Why in the world do you want to go there?' he asked. 'You'll just get a stiff neck from looking at all those tall trees!' "

We turned off the road and waded hip-deep along a trail, Fran cautioning me to walk directly behind him. "You can't see streambeds or tree roots under the water," he noted. Several dozen yards farther on we came to a submerged boardwalk; at its end an overlook stood before a large opening in the flooded forest. "Welcome to Weston Lake," Fran said. It was the only underwater lake I had ever seen!

Wading through deep water tested seldom-used muscles, and I gratefully accepted the invitation of park ranger Guy Taylor to accompany him on a motorboat trip on Cedar Creek, in the northern and eastern parts of the monument. A slender, wiry man wearing dark-rimmed glasses, Guy steered the battered green aluminum johnboat with the ease of long experience. For the most part we followed the course of Cedar Creek, but I soon found myself unable to distinguish the twisting, looping creek from the many smaller streams running into it. "You get lost in here," said Guy, "and you are the *lostest* lost!"

Occasionally we found our way blocked by a floating log, and when there wasn't a clear way around it, Guy gunned the outboard motor and headed straight

BALD CYPRESS
Taxodium distichum

toward it, humping the slanted prow over the obstruction. As we slid over the log, Guy backed off on the throttle and tilted the engine forward so the propeller would clear. When we were over, he eased the motor back down and revved it up again —as neat a job of log-jumping as you could ask for.

Several times, Guy and I heard the hoot of the barred owl—"Who cooks for you, who cooks for you, who cooks for you all?" it called. Then I spotted one of the birds perched in a bald cypress. It sat peering at us as Guy swung the boat around and maneuvered among the trees to get closer. We watched the owl for several minutes before it flew off. "I don't know whether the shade's so deep or there just haven't been many people in the swamp," said Guy. "But the owls hoot all day long in here. Most places, I have only heard them at night."

Farther on, we entered a part of the monument where turn-of-the-century loggers had cut most of the mature cypresses. Guy pointed out one they had missed. Its gaunt skeleton, bleached white, rose amid the bright green of the forest canopy. "The loggers would wait until the swamp flooded," he explained. "Then they would come in boats and girdle the trees they wanted. The following summer, when the dense cypress wood had dried out enough to float, teams of men would saw the trees down and float the logs to the river." He pointed out the ax marks circling the dead tree. "Look at that. That tree's been standing there for three-quarters of a century, and the wood's as solid as the day it was cut. It won't even rot."

Guy pointed out the difference between the trunks of the bald cypress and the water tupelo. Both trees' bases are buttressed, but the cypress has deeper indentations. He plucked a leaf from a swamp cottonwood to show how it grows slightly more heart-shaped than the regular cottonwood. On a low branch in a nearby tree lay the nest of a yellow-crowned night-heron, just a few sticks in a haphazard arrangement, too sparse, it seemed, to support eggs or chicks.

Near Cedar Creek I saw a national champion overcup oak. This water-loving species takes its name from the acorns it produces, whose caps nearly enclose the fruit. A majestic specimen, the champion stood 148 feet tall, its trunk more than 22 feet around. Sunlight filtered through its crown like shafts of light probing the dark of an ancient cathedral.

To give my feet a chance to dry out, I wandered along the boardwalk being built near the visitor center at Congaree. The walkway begins on the slopes leading down to the floodplain, amid a carpet of ferns—cinnamon fern, with its tall spore stalk; low-growing southern lady fern; royal fern; and netted chain fern, named for the chainlike convolutions of its fertile stalk.

Near the boardwalk, forest tent caterpillars inched along branches and fell from the trees, fuzzy gray creatures with almost incandescent blue and yellow markings. A gray tree frog sat immobile on the walkway railing as I quietly edged past. Poison ivy vines as thick as my arm, their dense covering of hairlike rootlets indicating great age, clung to massive tree trunks.

Among the towering oaks and pines grew climbing hydrangea and trees called "musclewood." I knew the latter as ironwood. I'd seen the trees growing in the Ohio woodlots I wandered as a boy. The ones I recalled were spindly things just a few inches thick; here they were real trees, their smooth bark covering trunks nearly a foot across.

I spotted a red-bellied water snake lying motionless on a log. A smooth skink disappeared in a flash between the cracks of the boardwalk, then peeked back from the safety of a supporting post. A few feet farther on, I watched a southern marbled salamander, its black four-inch-long body blotched with white, scurry along a branch sticking out of the water.

"We don't really know how many different kinds of plants and animals are in the monument," Fran Rametta told me. "No one has yet done a complete survey. We do know that the number keeps increasing, as people identify types we didn't know we had. There may be some other species out there, just waiting for someone to find them."

Noxubee National Wildlife Refuge, the last woodland I visited, was unlike any forest I'd seen so far. Located in east-central Mississippi, Noxubee is not renowned for its virgin timber, and the whine of the chain saw regularly sounds through its trees.

The refuge's bottomlands and ridges, covered with pines, hardwoods, and mixed stands, appear far different today from the way they did in the mid-1930s, when the Resettlement Administration bought the 46,000 acres of worn-out land from farmers who were just as exhausted. At first, the government couldn't find one of its own agencies to take over the nearly worthless acreage. Finally, in 1940, the U. S. Fish and Wildlife Service agreed to manage the property as a refuge and began a reforestation program.

"We have four major objectives here," refuge manager Jim Tisdale explained, ticking them off on his fingers. "First, to care for endangered species. Second, to benefit waterfowl. Third, to create a good environment for other wildlife, such as deer, turkeys, birds—the whole works. Fourth, to provide for public enjoyment of what we have here."

With chief forester Craig Hays, I set off to see the refuge. Near the Noxubee River, a narrow, shallow stream running gently between six-foot-high clay banks, we walked through a stand of hardwoods—ash, oak, shagbark hickory. Widely spaced, straight and true, the huge trees stood. Craig kicked a low stump with his toe and remarked, "You wouldn't know this was logged just last year, would you?"

I was surprised. Where were the broken younger trees, the skidder tracks, the tops and branches trimmed from the trunks? Why could I see several dead trees from where I stood? This didn't look at all like any other logged forest I had seen.

Craig grinned. "We keep a close eye on logging operations here. And we've got pretty good contractors taking the timber. They realize it's to their benefit, as well as ours, if they do a careful job. We like them to cut close to the ground, for example, and they do. That way, there aren't a lot of stumps to mess up their trucks the next time they cut this stand.

"The fewer standing trees they skin up, the better the quality of the next harvest. And to remove the slash, we opened this stand for firewood cutting after the loggers finished—only for the downed stuff, of course. People got free wood, and we got a nice, clean forest floor.

"Those dead trees that you see provide homes for many animals, so we leave them standing. Every fall, we flood the stand. It makes a great habitat for wood ducks."

Craig summed up the refuge's management philosophy. "We use logging here as a tool to encourage diversity. We do a lot of selective cutting, marking trees for harvesting in order to open up the forest canopy.

"Give me a chain saw and a box of matches," declared Craig, "and I'll give you a better forest!"

One morning I watched Leon Fuller, a local logger, improving a stand by chain saw. Earlier, Craig had inventoried the stand, marking trees to be cut with spots of bright orange paint. It was a mixed stand about 40 years old, mostly pines but with a few hardwoods. The canopy high above had grown together, darkening the floor and decreasing the green cover growing there. Felling the marked trees would create openings for sunlight, increasing the amount of cover and food for wildlife and creating a more healthful environment for tree seedlings.

Leon Fuller has been logging for at least 35 of his 56 years, he told me. Today he was doing it pretty much the way he did when he started. Fuller was using Dave and Doc, a team of mules, to skid the logs from where they were cut to his "Logger's Dream" side-loading truck.

Two other men, George Harrington and Henry Ford—Henry's nickname was Model T—worked with Leon. George did most of the felling, topped the trunks, trimmed off branches, and cut the logs to mill length. Henry tended the mules and helped load the truck. Leon drove the truck and supervised. At least that was how Leon described the roles to me. Actually, everybody did whatever needed to be done.

When a tree was down, topped, and trimmed, Henry (or Leon, or George) walked the mules over to the log and turned them into position so he could grab the log with tongs hanging from the doubletree behind the mules. On command, Dave and Doc leaned into the harness and dragged the log over to the loading area.

"I like mules," Leon remarked. "Those two are pretty good workers. We could probably do this about three times as fast if we used a skidder. But it would tear up the woods a lot more."

"Yes, sir. This is going to be a real pretty stand of timber some day."

After having visited forests where the entire emphasis was on preservation, not harvesting, it took me awhile to get used to Craig's view of the woods as a resource to be managed. But time and again, he showed me how well the policy was working at Noxubee. I was impressed by how often he used the word "aesthetically," as in "We made the outline of this field irregular. It not only gives us more edge effect—the prime habitat where different environments meet—but also makes the view more aesthetically pleasing."

A forester through and through, Craig is a concerned and intelligent man, able to balance the many claims on his woodlands. One of the major claims is made not by loggers, hunters, or other humans. It is made by the red-cockaded woodpecker.

This rare bird, on the endangered species list since 1970, has a number of peculiarities that have hastened its decline. The woodpeckers nest in clans of usually two to five birds, but only one pair mates and produces young. And the red-cockaded is particular about its nesting site. It generally chips cavities in older living pines that have red heart, a disease that softens the trees' heartwood and gives it a reddish tinge.

Even when all other conditions are right, if the forest understory grows up near nest height, the birds abandon the site. And other woodpeckers, such as the red-headed and even the large pileated, sometimes take over the red-cockaded's cavities and enlarge them for their own use, driving out the smaller birds.

Near the headquarters of the refuge, I watched a red-cockaded carving out a nest in a loblolly pine. Through binoculars, I could see the chips falling as the bird perched on the rim of the hole. Its head disappeared each time it bent to its task. Every 15 or 20 minutes it would fly off, but invariably it would soon return.

Once another red-cockaded flew down and clung to the trunk near the new nest hole. The first bird backed away from its work and the newcomer looked in. After a thorough inspection and a few half-hearted pecks, it flew away and the other bird went back to its work.

Craig told me that increasing logging has left fewer and fewer habitats for red-cockaded woodpeckers. The 14 known active colonies at Noxubee, however, have several areas in which to live. Craig makes sure of that. He not only preserves the stands they are known to frequent, but he also finds and manages other likely nesting sites, areas where trees with red heart are growing.

"It can take one of the birds two years to finish chipping out a nest hole," he told me. "If something happens that makes the birds leave that area, there aren't many places for them to go. Besides needing a particular type of habitat, the red-cockaded needs a lot of it. A clan's average home range is about 200 acres. Maybe we're supporting as many birds as possible. But until we find out for sure, we're going to do whatever we can to help the red-cockaded along."

One afternoon Craig and I walked through a section of the refuge proposed for inclusion in the federal wilderness system. In this area, no logging was permitted; nature followed its own course. As we hiked among stands of papaws growing under mature cherrybark oaks, hickories, and sweet gums, Craig waved his hand at the leaf-littered gray of the forest floor.

"See how different this is? Hardly anything's growing here, compared to the rest of the refuge. I know that places like this are getting fewer and fewer all the time, and we ought to preserve them. I support that. But I just can't help wishing once in a while I could bring a chain saw in here and open up that canopy a little bit!"

When I left Noxubee, I carried with me an answer to a question that had troubled me throughout my travels: How can we harvest timber from our woodlands and yet maintain these complex ecosystems? One solution is the intelligent use of forests as practiced at Noxubee National Wildlife Refuge.

"We spent a great deal of time bringing the timber up to where it is," Jim Tisdale told me. "Now it's in pretty good shape." I had to agree. It is in good shape now. Here, on land once ravaged by erosion and too worn out to farm, the refuge sells from a quarter to half a million dollars' worth of timber every year. But more important, it has brought back a living forest, a green, diverse world that is home to an abundance of wild creatures.

WATER TUPELO
Nyssa aquatica

99

Alert five-inch Carolina anole (right) peeks over the edge of a pickerelweed leaf at the National Audubon Society's Corkscrew Swamp Sanctuary in southwestern Florida. Home to an abundance of plant and animal life, this 11,000-acre wilderness preserves the largest virgin stand of bald cypress in the United States. At left, a bee lands on a pickerelweed blossom. An anole clings to the stalk below. Erroneously called American chameleons—they actually belong to a different family— these lizards change their color from green to brown according to emotional state, light, and temperature, not simply to match their surroundings. Below, spidery bracts curl from the stem of a wild hibiscus blooming in a patch of sun.

PRECEDING PAGES: Airboat cruises through saw grass and cabbage palmettos in Big Cypress Swamp, a watery realm that includes Corkscrew Swamp Sanctuary. Other environments typical of the southern region include upland pine woodlands, deciduous forests, and mixed broadleaf-conifer stands.

*R*are Florida panther
perches in a bald cypress in
Big Cypress National
Preserve. Below the panther,
spiky fronds of cabbage
palmetto fan upward. Brown
tufts of bromeliads, or air
plants, cling to the cypress
branches beyond. In 1982,
officials named the
endangered panther the state
animal after Florida
schoolchildren voted it their
favorite wild creature. A
subspecies of the mountain
lion or cougar of the western
United States, the panther
lives precariously in a
shrunken habitat. Sightings
occur so infrequently in Big
Cypress that biologists
studying the elusive animals
cannot reliably estimate
their numbers.

PETER B. GALLAGHER

*T*hree-week-old alligators hitch a ride on their mother's back in Corkscrew Swamp Sanctuary. There the babies find safety from predators such as raccoons, birds, and other gators. At an environmental education center in nearby Big Cypress Preserve, visitors observe alligators and other threatened or endangered species. In a mock hearing (right), sixth graders assume the roles of developers, farmers, and park rangers—competitors for southern Florida's water supply. Classmates acting as judges (opposite, lower) weigh the testimony before announcing their decision: This time the rangers and the wildlife win.

Lush mosses and lichens green the stump of a fallen oak in Congaree Swamp National Monument near Columbia, South Carolina. Inundated an average of ten times a year, the preserve supports a wide range of water-tolerant trees and a cornucopia of animal life not yet fully cataloged. Much of the monument has never heard the ring of the logger's ax. At upper left, adhesive pads on its toes help a gray tree frog hold tight to an American holly. Forest tent caterpillars (left, center) crawl along the back of a brown water snake. Monument officials have so far recorded 15 species of snakes in Congaree Swamp. Near the park's entrance, a snapping turtle (below) opens a beak powerful enough to sever a finger.

Barren limbs of a forest giant accent the thick canopy of century-old trees in a seldom-visited portion of Congaree Swamp. Along the floodplain of the Congaree River, such trees as oaks, tupelos, and elms crowd together. At higher elevations, the drier ground supports species such as beech and pine. Below, fallen leaves lie scattered among roots of an American beech. At right, vines of catbrier, Virginia creeper, and climbing hydrangea cling to a loblolly pine. Green lichens nurtured by the hot, humid atmosphere edge the scaly bark that identifies this typically southern conifer.

FOLLOWING PAGES: *Draped sinuously in the branches of a tree, a nonpoisonous rat snake suns itself in Big Thicket National Preserve, an 84,550-acre woodland sanctuary near Beaumont, Texas.*

*B*ald cypress trees flourish in a slough in the Neches River floodplain, one of the varied habitats in Big Thicket National Preserve. Knobby, pointed cypress knees poke up from the water near the fluted trunks. Botanists hold differing theories about the function of these porous root growths. Some believe they may transport oxygen to root systems. At right, a great egret soars on broad wings in the Big Thicket region. Another egret (opposite, bottom) guards its nest; inside, a downy chick demands food with a grating kak-kak-kak.

Children at Camp Niwana, near the Big Thicket Preserve, clamber about an ancient southern magnolia known as the Chapel Tree. Its roots serve as a gathering place for outdoor services at the Camp Fire Council facility. Plants large and small thrive in the Big Thicket. Below, fragrant swamp spider lilies flower amid the humid reek of rotting vegetation in a Neches River slough. On the poorly drained soils of wetland savannas, minuscule sundews (upper right) exude sticky droplets to catch insects on matchhead-size tentacles; tubular leaves of pitcher plants (lower right) contain pools of enzymes that digest insects trapped inside by downward-pointing hairs.

*I*ts future hanging in the balance, a red-cockaded woodpecker chick some 20 days old weighs in at about 38 grams—less than an ounce and a half. At east-central Mississippi's Noxubee National Wildlife Refuge, scientists weigh and band the endangered birds as part of an ongoing study. The red-cockaded's numbers have declined steadily as its woodland habitat has shrunk. Increased timber harvesting has reduced suitable nesting trees. A tame woodpecker named Lady Red (above, right) reaches for a tidbit of cricket proffered by Dr. Jerome A. Jackson of Mississippi State University, an authority on the red-cockaded. Above, left, Lady Red clings to a loblolly pine. Rescued as a fledgling with a broken wing and leg, since mended, the bird cannot fly well enough for release into the wild. Dr. Jackson, who has studied Lady Red's development and behavior, uses her as a lure to capture other woodpeckers for banding and measuring. "In such cases we refer to her as Tokyo Rose," he says. Dr. Jackson's experiences with Lady Red may provide valuable insights into captive breeding should that become necessary.

*D*ewdrops spangle blossoms of Queen Anne's lace and drooping cheat grass in Noxubee National Wildlife Refuge. Above, a June sun burns mist from Bluff Lake. Offering one example of sound forestry practices, the 46,230-acre refuge pursues the goals of producing both a sustained annual harvest of timber and an increasing wealth of wildlife.

Backcountry Wonderlands

By Jane R. McCauley

QUAKING ASPEN
Populus tremuloides

THE RED MASS FLAMES and billows across the darkening sky. Gusty winds batter the woodland, blanketed in ash in every direction. Permeating the air, the acrid odor of pine burns the lungs. Eyes water. Bodies sweat. Crackling and snapping, decades-old trees bow, submitting to their fate. It seems, without a doubt, that no living thing will survive this holocaust.

Late in the afternoon, a black cloud opens, spilling forth drenching rain. When darkness falls, the winds abate, and temperatures plunge steadily. Weary men and women in yellow hard hats, their faces smeared with soot, file down the slopes. For days they have battled the inferno. As dawn breaks, the rain strengthens. Finally, for a while at least, the fury is relenting.

I am standing on a hillside outside Helena, Montana, watching this nightmare unfold. It is summer, late August of 1984. Nearly 27,000 acres in or near the Helena National Forest and the Gates of the Mountains Wilderness are ablaze. This is the North Hill fire, second largest of 18 raging across the state. The tragedy began four days ago. In response, more than eight thousand fire fighters have rushed to the sites from 11 states.

The scene here is terrifying. The blazes have fanned out rapidly in winds at times exceeding 50 miles per hour, forcing evacuation of communities, destroying homes, and creating havoc for crews. One of the fire fighters assigned to North Hill, a young woman from California, her eyes blurred by fatigue, says to me, "You'd better believe it's scary out there. Once, that wind shifted and we thought we were going to have to get into our fireproof tents. That's really a last resort."

Fire. It is, I would learn, one of the strongest natural forces shaping the forests of the Rocky Mountains. From Canada south to Mexico, vast stands of fir, spruce, juniper, pine, and aspen spread over the Rockies. Variations in elevation, slope exposure, moisture, and soil determine the densities and distribution of the trees. Rugged, remote terrain and late, sparse settlement—along with wilderness preservation efforts—have kept many of these woodlands primeval, far longer than those to the east.

And, for something like 10,000 years, intermittent wildfires have raced up these forested slopes, leaving little in their wake. Ironically, these devastating fires have actually perpetuated certain plant and animal species, and ultimately, the very forests themselves.

At the Helena Interagency Fire Control Center, representatives from the state of Montana, the Forest Service, the Bureau of Land Management, and the National Guard were meeting day and night to plan fire control measures. A calmness prevailed, I observed, despite the commotion. Just outside, trailers, tents, and helicopters cluttered the makeshift campground set up for fire fighters working 14-hour shifts. Using infrared scanners, officials monitored hot spots. With computer models of terrain and weather patterns, experts charted the burn's projected course.

"We're assembling all this data continuously to plan our day-by-day action," said Forest Service fire manager Sonny Stiger as he slumped exhausted into the chair next to me. "Whatever we do, we have to weigh the cost, probability of loss of life, and wilderness impact. Right now we're trying to decide whether to put smoke jumpers in here." He spread a map before us, pointing to Mann Gulch, a corner of the Gates of the Mountains Wilderness. "Thirteen fire fighters were killed in that steep terrain in 1949. We're not forgetting that."

When, some ten days later, officials declare that all 18 blazes have been contained, more than 200,000 acres lie charred and blackened across the state. The cost is high: One life, that of a volunteer fireman, is lost; damage exceeds 14 million dollars.

"There's a lesson in all this," said Sonny. "Prescribed burns over the last decades could have prevented a fire of this intensity." The issue of prescribed burns has been debated for years. Sonny explained his remark.

"The primary vegetation here is ponderosa pine and Douglas fir," he said, "two types of trees that normally burn without man's interference every five to thirty years. This is nature's way of keeping the fuels down." Sonny added that low intensity fire, as in a prescribed burn, inflicts little damage on ponderosa pines. The thick bark of the pines helps protect the trees, enabling them to withstand the heat.

"Now the woods are full of spruce budworm, trees are dying, and the deadwood is so thick you can't get through it. If we'd allowed prescribed burns, nature would have created stands of healthy trees and lush grasses."

Research forester Dr. James Lotan elaborated on the prescribed burn issue when I met him at the Northern Forest Fire Lab in Missoula. This city is the hub of forestry for the northern Rockies. "Until the 1970s," he said, "the attitude in the Forest Service, and of most people, was that all fire is bad. Then the policy began shifting away from strict protectionism, and in 1978 the Forest Service adopted a policy permitting prescribed burns to be set in every area but designated wilderness." "What about now?" I asked. "As of February 1985, we're allowed to set fires in wilderness areas, too, when tinder reaches explosive levels."

Jim explained how an area's fire history can be traced through the levels of charcoal in the soil and through charred sections in growth rings. Investigators use such information to forecast a prescribed fire's potential impact on an area. "We know, for example, that massive crown fires—the ones that rip through the tops of trees—occurred every 200 to 300 years in the higher elevations of spruce and lodgepole pine."

Other than clearing slash, I wondered what were the benefits of prescribed blazes. A list tumbled from Jim. "Many species that are unable to reseed in shade, such as most pines and larches, will germinate in areas cleared by fire. Other types that are adapted to fire, such as lodgepole pines, have cones that require heat to open and scatter their seeds. Then, too, fires release stored nutrients into the soil at a faster rate." Jim added that even natural fires can be managed to produce the beneficial effects of a prescribed burn.

Neither Jim nor Sonny had mentioned the effect of fire on wildlife. When I asked, Jim admitted that fires do destroy some animals in the ecosystem, but he reassured me that many others, such as moose and elk, actually benefit from the spurts of new plant growth a burn often stimulates. "Fire's really a double-edged sword," said Jim. "It's both a destroyer and a giver of life."

Snow still dusted the peaks as I headed farther north, following the Canadian Rockies through a succession of picture-perfect parks. The mountains here loom more rugged, more massive than their southern counterparts, although many rise little more than 10,000 feet. Geologically speaking, this region is young. Just 15,000 years ago, ice covered most of the Canadian Rockies. As the ice receded, it left behind deep valleys and startling aquamarine lakes, some stretching for ten miles. Tiers of bluish green spruce and lighter fir press close to the lakeshores. Waterfalls sing liltingly over layers of sedimentary rock. Streams whisper past a changing palette of wildflowers.

The tree species that now thrive here spread northward following the last ice age. Larch, lodgepole pine, and birch spread quickly; other pines, spruce, and fir more slowly. These woodlands are volatile, and fire, avalanche, flood, even wind, promise change. Lodgepole pines move in and capture meadows. In time, smothered by their own shade, the lodgepoles give way to spruce and fir.

In some areas the struggle for light, like the fight for water in a desert, is so intense that the woods can seem almost desolate, offering little hint of the wildlife within. Yet a patient observer may be rewarded with such glories as mule deer, moose, even grizzly bears. I soon discovered, however, that a face-to-face meeting with a grizzly can be disconcerting.

Ambling down a trail at twilight outside Banff National Park, I nearly stumbled into a cinnamon grizzly and her cub, which were foraging at the edge of a thicket not far from the Bow River. The distinctive hump between the bears' shoulder blades identified them as grizzlies. The 300-pound female eyed me warily as she chewed a mouthful of berries. I felt like an intruder. Then I, too, eyed her, realizing to my dismay that she was not more than a few dozen yards away. Suddenly I no longer regarded bears as docile creatures like the one that comforted me through my childhood, that tattered teddy now locked away in a dusty old trunk. An out-of-sorts grizzly may charge, maiming, even killing.

Blessedly, this encounter ended uneventfully. The grizzly continued munching; I crossed my fingers, eased by her quietly, then quickened my pace to the safety of my car. Whew! Earlier this same day officials had closed a trail in the park after a bear harassed campers. Rangers captured the bear, then moved it to the remote interior of the nearby Siffleur Wilderness Area.

In fact, grizzly-human confrontations were up during the summer throughout the northern Rockies: a July mauling in Yellowstone National Park, the first reported death in the park since 1972; a bear invading a Laundromat; one charging and mauling a California woman hiking a popular backcountry trail in Montana's Glacier National Park. A Wyoming lodge owner told me she and her husband have been bothered so often by bears that they now drive the short distance between their cabins in spring and fall. She worries that other people aren't cautious enough.

Why the recent problems? Dr. Charles Jonkel, director of the Border Grizzly Project in Missoula, believes there just isn't enough food for them this year. "Both Dick Knight, a colleague who directs the Interagency Grizzly Bear Study Team, and I have been saying this would happen. Three foods the bears depend on—the huckleberry, the whitebark pine nut, and the buffalo berry—are not available." Dr. Jonkel pointed out that no one knows why these foods are scarce, but some are blaming it on the early, lasting cold snap in the fall of 1983.

Once widespread across western North America, the grizzly was placed on the threatened species list in 1975 when hunting, loss of habitat to logging, and the killing of nuisance bears threatened it with extinction. Now, under federal protection, the bears are reviving. But as people encroach farther into the woods, maintaining sufficient habitat for the bears remains a serious problem. For the past 11 years, Dr. Jonkel and his group have studied "brother griz," its environment, and people's attitudes. They are also experimenting with substances to keep bears away from humans, such as a powerful red pepper derivative.

One question is central. Should people have priority over wildlife in wilderness areas? The laws say no. While strongly worded pamphlets caution visitors about grizzlies, they also advise that the bears are a natural part of the environment. One effort to ensure a balanced ecosystem involves members of five federal agencies and the fish and game departments of four states. Called the Interagency Grizzly Bear Committee, this group oversees grizzly habitat, at times designating backcountry areas from which people should be banned.

Considering the volume of park visitors, however, bear incidents aren't that frequent. Many backwoods hikers I talked with believe the possibility of bear encounters is just one of the risks that go with a wilderness experience. One thing is certain: These woodland kings have caused concern for a long time. Indians, fur trappers, and early cattlemen related terrifying tales about the bears. Even the intrepid explorers Lewis and Clark were awed by grizzlies, filling long pages in their journals with accounts of hairbreadth getaways.

Many of Lewis and Clark's adventures took place along the Lolo Trail, which winds for roughly a hundred miles from Lolo, Montana, to Weippe, Idaho, passing through the spreading conifers of the Lolo and Clearwater National Forests. In their search for a river route to the Pacific, Lewis and Clark crossed the trail in 1805 and returned east along it in 1806, the first white men known to do so. A century before their travel here, Indians were padding along the trail on the way

DOUGLAS FIR
Pseudotsuga menziesii

to the buffalo herds in the Montana and Wyoming region.

The story of the Lolo Trail recounted by Lewis and Clark is one of hazards—of blinding snowstorms, timber-strewn passages, horses toppling on slippery paths, and near starvation. My tale, on the other hand, is one of clear running streams, hot springs, and enchanting forests. I still carry their memories.

Today a two-lane highway, Route 12, parallels what is left of the original Lolo Trail. On the south side of the road flows the river aptly named the Lochsa, the Flathead Indian word for rough water. Above the river, spires of the Bitterroots etch a craggy skyline. A drive along this winding road from Montana to Idaho dramatically reveals the transition from a dry mountain forest to a moist woodland that is more characteristic of the Pacific coast.

In his office at the University of Montana's School of Forestry, in Missoula, Dr. Robert Pfister described the diversity of vegetation along Route 12. A former Forest Service scientist who now devotes all his time to research, Dr. Pfister is a well-known authority on western woodlands. Maps and technical journals, many his work or that of his colleagues, papered the table in front of us.

"At this end of the road, you'll see the typical Montana vegetation—widely spaced ponderosa pines with grasses and shrubs, dense Douglas firs and western larches, then lodgepole pine and subalpine fir when you get above 4,000 feet." Water, slope, and elevation determine the tree species as well as their prevalence. "You'll see how sparse the pines are on the exposed south-facing slopes. Contrast them with the dense stands of Douglas firs on the north-facing slopes."

To the west of Missoula, beyond 5,233-foot Lolo Pass, 30 to 50 inches of precipitation falls annually, nourishing a near-maritime forest. "The trees there are really miniature versions of those monarchs found on the Pacific coast," Dr. Pfister told me. "You get growth rates nearly double those in drier areas. Western red cedar, western hemlock, western white pine, and grand fir all flourish. You'll also see many more plants in the undergrowth." As he rushed off to another appointment, he smiled and said, "Why don't you go explore that Route 12. I think you'll find it spectacular."

To really know a woodland is to take to its trails on foot. I had sampled dry mountain forests in Montana and in Canada. Now I set out to ramble through those lush forests beyond Lolo Pass that Dr. Pfister had described. Shouldering my pack, I pushed into the woods and was immediately confronted by large numbers of decomposing logs scattered on hillsides and across the trail. Such logs had also troubled Lewis and Clark, I consoled myself. Saplings grew amid their decay. The air felt cool, humid.

As I whiffed the fragrance of cedar, the beauty of this place struck me, uplifting me like a glimpse of the sun after endless cloudy days. Spongy chartreuse mosses, clusters of tan mushrooms, deep green pine needles, and white Indian pipes matted the damp earth. Orange lichens splattered rocks, climbed blackish-brown trunks; grayish-green old-man's beard dangled in swags from branches. Delicate maidenhair ferns reached out and tickled me. Bending down, I picked up the chubby cone of a Douglas fir. Diminutive three-pronged forks stuck out between the scales.

At elevations below 4,000 feet, larches and pines intermingled with western red cedar. I ran my hand up and down the stringy bark of a cedar; its long, shallow roots spread across the path. Penetrating the canopy above, bleached dead limbs reached upward, laced by cobwebs. Just then the wind moaned, a sprinkle of rain fell, and I trembled, somewhat spooked. Hot springs bubbled up from the floor of a clearing ahead. I eased into one and reflected on the softness and mellowness of this forest. How different it seemed from others I had visited where

the struggle for water is harsher. I soaked up its transcendent peace.

Along this portion of the trail, I saw no large animals. No matter. Every forested acre here is home to hosts of smaller ones. Perched above a brook on an uprooted cedar, I watched a miniature parade of these creatures. A chipmunk scurried about, chasing sunbeams along the ground. The brook chattered, coaxing a water strider across it. A jay's screeching sounded overhead.

Soon, an iridescent blue dragonfly landed near me, shedding its shyness and coming close . . . then closer. Determined to disturb it, a bee buzzed within an inch of its head. I packed up my gear and slowly moved on, glancing back. The bee was still hovering like a toy helicopter.

Its rotors rapidly gaining momentum, the flashy red-and-white chopper lifted straight up, turned right, then headed away from us toward a distant slope where ponderosa pines, Douglas firs, and grand firs climbed in ranks like soldiers in green fatigues. A steel cable reached 200 feet toward the ground below. Sweeping back and forth, it reminded me of a clock's pendulum. Having turned my back to escape the helicopter's blast, I faced around as the whine of chain saws reached my ears.

At my side, Jon Baxter, pilot for Columbia Helicopters, shouted to me. "Four pilots, three mechanics, and twenty-two loggers are involved. That wood up there's mighty heavy." We were standing at a Boise Cascade logging site some four air miles west of Donnelly, in Idaho's Boise National Forest. I looked at my watch. Ready. Set. Go. In a finely tuned sequence, the Boeing Vertol 107 picked up three or four logs, headed downhill, then dropped them at a landing area. Three minutes exactly. Seconds count in this business.

Helicopters are one of the most recent innovations—first used successfully in the early 1970s—in logging the forests of the Rockies, and with them has come the ability to fell timber rapidly and efficiently on formerly inaccessible slopes. Scattered stands are removed without the necessity of relocating heavy machinery. Some environmentalists praise the use of helicopters because they do not cause serious soil disturbance, and they reduce the need for erosion-causing roads.

"It's an early '60s passenger helicopter that's been stripped down," Jon explained. "It can carry up to 10,500 pounds." He added that the 6,000-foot elevation of this site reduced the lift capacity to 9,000 pounds. The pilot's voice droned over the radio Jon carried: "I've got you in sight, but I'm just trying to control the ship here in this wind."

As we strolled across a meadow, Jon described how the pilot must hold the chopper steady enough to allow the men on the ground to attach the logs to the cable's hook. Problems can arise. High winds can keep the cable flying out of reach, and the cable can break. "While one man hooks on the logs," Jon gestured with his hands, "five others are preparing the next load. Before the pilot lifts off, he's got to make sure he knows where all six men are." Amid the radio's crackling, I hear, "Where are you?" "I've got you now." "This one's a 5,400-pounder."

Seconds later, the Vertol dropped its cargo at the landing area, where checkered shirted "chasers," yellow hard hats shading their leathery faces, yanked off the chokers holding the logs. "Knot bumpers" inspected the logs, then swiftly lopped off the limbs just moments before a front-end loader neatly stacked them. There's little time for talk, but one long-time woodsman, the stature of Paul Bunyan, chatted with me. "People say we're the ones who go where most loggers won't. I like it because we're always movin', and we get into the real stuff . . . the big, inaccessible wood."

In the latter 1800s, when much of the virgin forest farther east had disappeared, lumberjacks pushed west, first

WESTERN LARCH
Larix occidentalis

to the Pacific coast, then back to the Rockies. Logging companies sprang up as the need for wood for railroads, mines, and towns grew. Traveling through the northern Rockies today, one is never without a sense of near-continuous harvesting. In Missoula, Montana, a logging truck rolls into town every four minutes bound for one of several mills. At Christmastime, strings of railroad cars head east stacked with Douglas firs.

Despite changes in technology, the spirit of the frontier lives on in a few stalwart woodsmen who cling to the time-honored method of horse logging. "Gee . . . haw." "All right now, boys." "Turn around." "Seems I'm only half in control here. These animals have a mind of their own." His Stetson bobbed up and down as Woody Barmore straddled the slanting bundle of logs and eased the two Belgian horses into the loading area amid the yaps of Fair, his partner's friendly dog. "Whoa, boys." The animals stood motionless. Within five minutes, he had separated the logs, one stack for firewood, others for fence posts and poles.

"We've been working on this sale, about 750,000 board feet, since last fall." "Mostly lodgepole," I ventured. "Yup." "How long you been at this?" "Oh, maybe five years."

Woody and his partner, Jack Malmberg, head up Double Tree Logging, one of Wyoming's few remaining horse-logging outfits and among the handful still operating in the northern Rockies. I caught up with the two men at Beaver Creek, a few miles outside Lander, as the setting sun emblazoned the sheer walls of the nearby Wind River Range. Wit, an iron constitution, and a profound respect for nature characterize both Woody and Jack.

"We're thinning here," Jack explained. "Most of these trees are about 60 to 80 years old." Hard to believe, I thought, as I looked around at the gangling pines, the majority no more than three to four inches across. "Look, I'll show you," Jack said, swiftly slicing a cross section from one and handing it to me. (A later count would reveal some one hundred growth rings.)

Fell. Buck. Stack. The work continued as we talked. "It's the four S's in this business," Jack said. "Sunup, sundown, Sundays, and then some." "Gotta love the mountains, hard work, and the woods," Woody added, reading my mind as I wondered why anyone would want to toil like this. "You'll be seeing more horses," he continued, pointing out that the animals are best for thinning operations, which help ensure successful regeneration. "Foresters today haven't had a chance to see what we can do with them. Anyway," he grinned, "with horses, we don't have to listen to the roar of diesels."

"Why are these trees so red?" I asked, walking toward one that looked as though someone had doused it with dye. "Mountain pine beetle," Jack said as he joined me. He peeled away the tree's scaly, gray-orange bark, revealing distinctive channels about an eighth of an inch wide. "The female carves these grooves for her eggs." Pitch oozed profusely from other pines, one of the first indicators of this usually terminal infestation.

An insidious bug, the mountain pine beetle has cut a wide swath across the Rockies from Colorado northward into Alberta, at times reaching epidemic levels. To learn more about this pest, I talked with Dr. Bob Averill, regional entomologist with the Forest Service in Denver, Colorado.

"Back in the 1970s," he said, "we had a large-scale outbreak in ponderosa pines. Now we have one in lodgepole pines." He explained that the insect—about the size of a match head—burrows under the bark, then lays its eggs. Two weeks later the eggs hatch into larvae that feed on the pine until the following summer. The larvae's damage kills the tree within a year.

Since the Forest Service has stopped

applying ethylene dibromide (EDB), the usual weapon in fighting the pine beetle, only two alternatives remain: clearcutting or thinning. The Forest Service has implemented increasing numbers of tree removals, even reaching into such resorts as Vail, Colorado. Developers fear that hillsides bared of pines could have a negative impact on the ski industry and on condominium sales. If such measures aren't taken, however, experts say the infestations will worsen.

Each year, millions of people flock to the recreation areas of the Rockies. They come to snowmobile or glide on freshly waxed skis through shadowy pathways in the pines, or to camp, fish, float rivers, or hunt. While timbering affairs have dominated in parts of the northern Rockies, recreation and water issues remain of concern in the central Rockies, especially in Colorado. In both economic and human terms, recreation may represent the single greatest value of Colorado's mountain forests.

Many sports centers—Aspen, Telluride, Silverton—endure as memorials to those who thronged here in the mid-1800s and later, seeking to wrench fortunes in silver and gold from these mountains. Skiers and hikers still pursue some of the woodland trails the prospectors blazed. In the heart of the once prospering mining area of west-central Colorado, I found scientists probing a range of mysteries at the Rocky Mountain Biological Laboratory, or RMBL. This field station's 205 acres sprawl within the Elk Mountains, whose peaks—several over 14,000 feet—are among Colorado's most commanding. Eight miles from the lab by a winding dirt road lies the ski resort town of Crested Butte.

Nourished by some 420 inches of snow each winter and abundant rainfall in summer, the lands surrounding RMBL harbor a rich diversity of flora and fauna. The terrain ranges from high desert to alpine; a thousand-foot climb is roughly equivalent to driving 600 miles north. Arrayed around the RMBL property are Gunnison National Forest, Maroon Bells-Snowmass Wilderness, and Gothic Natural Area—a tract of virgin spruce forest. These provide additional outlets for the students and faculty drawn from such esteemed universities as Cornell, Stanford, Harvard, and Northwestern.

One balmy Sunday afternoon, I sat with Dr. John C. Johnson, Jr., in the log cabin he and his wife, Dorothy, share here each summer. A zoologist from Pittsburg State University in Pittsburg, Kansas, Dr. Johnson served as RMBL's director for nine years. His father founded the lab in 1928 while a professor at Western State College in nearby Gunnison. As we sipped glasses of peppermint iced tea, Dr. Johnson recounted the area's early history. I felt myself stepping back to the turn of the century as I glanced around the cabin and at the faded black-and-white prints cluttering the mantel above the stone fireplace.

"There was a town here once, a typical Colorado silver boomtown called Gothic. The boom lasted from 1879 to 1881. The town, too, ended swiftly," he said, "when the veins didn't turn out to be as rich as expected, and transportation out of this remote area proved too difficult." A few wooden buildings still stand, looking, erroneously, as though one good shake would topple them. "Our newest addition," Dr. Johnson said proudly, "is a solar-assisted research laboratory, one with all the facilities of a lab in the middle of a city."

In our conversations, Dr. Johnson mentioned an esprit de corps that existed in the lab's early days. I found that spirit very much alive as I talked with students and professors during my stay. Studies here are varied. Among those that intrigued me: how hummingbirds adapt to high elevations; why only certain insects have evolved into pests; and the influence of color on the pollinators of scarlet gilia and purple larkspur.

One morning when the mountain air still held its bite, I seated myself on the library steps and listened to Dirk Van Vuren, whose thesis work on marmots has lured him back here for the past three summers. Cow parsnips and vetch glistened with dew at my feet. I felt humbled, as though inside a temple, with the colossal mountains and the pure fields all around me.

"I share a kinship with marmots by now," Dirk said, explaining how he tags them, surgically implants radio transmitters, then uses a receiver to track them. Closely related to woodchucks, marmots live in colonies, building networks of underground tunnels. They are hibernators, and one species—the yellow-bellied marmot—abounds in the Rockies. Dirk told me the young are born in early summer. Nearly half the females remain near their mothers, while all the males leave the colony when they are yearlings. Where the males disappear to is a question that has confounded biologists for years.

"I've implanted radio transmitters in 33 animals to try to answer that question," Dirk said. The transmitters he designed reach over a mile and will last, he hopes, for two years. "We have these restless animals," he mused, "like kids who grow up and think they've got to leave home. But we just don't know why." As I left him, he was heading back out, receiver in hand.

A few miles' drive and an hour's hike north of Gothic lies the 430-acre Mexican Cut, a preserve owned by the Nature Conservancy and administered by RMBL. Citing its research value, Colorado designated the Mexican Cut as its first scientific natural area in 1978. Both the area's isolation and the lab's ongoing efforts to control access have kept the Cut largely untouched, its forests climax.

I sensed the preserve's sacredness as I climbed the old wagon road leading into it. Accompanying me were Dr. Ruth Willey—Scottie—her husband, Bob, and Dennis Johns, RMBL's associate director.

Scottie and Bob promoted the purchase of the Mexican Cut. Scottie lost no time in transmitting her love for the area to me. Her bountiful energy often turns a walk into a run, and I hurried along to keep pace with her. Winter was still evident, and we skirted lingering patches of snow.

"Any disturbance can upset the balance here," she said. "That's why we have left the entrance barricaded with fallen trees. Even our own people walk in. We also hold the water rights, and, therefore, have been able to prevent pollution."

A basin scooped into the side of a mountain by a small glacier, the preserve climbs to 12,580 feet. As we ascended a series of benches, we passed through a distinct zone of Engelmann spruce and subalpine fir, which finally gave way to treeless tundra. For centuries, succession has gone on here virtually undisturbed. Linked together like a strand of beads, 17 ponds stairstep down to 11,000 feet. Because their elevations and drainage patterns vary, each one holds diverse and unique life forms—a natural laboratory.

Wildflowers—magenta violets, pink spring beauties, blue columbine—dazzled me as we moved from one motionless pond to another. Scottie scooped out a handful of water from pond eight. It teemed with tiny fairy shrimp and copepods. From another, she collected a salamander. Very few baby salamanders have appeared in the ponds in the past two years. There is some speculation that acid rain is the culprit.

Professor John Harte of the University of California at Berkeley emphasizes that more research is needed to pinpoint the cause. Harte and his team have monitored acid rain levels in the preserve over the past five years. Despite the Cut's remoteness from industrial centers, the precipitation falling here has been found to be surprisingly acidic.

I thought about this disturbing news as we turned back, heading down through the forest now brooding in afternoon's lengthening shadows. We can keep out man, but still his pollutants seep in.

Leaving the Mexican Cut—as pristine a place as I have ever seen—I paused for a soda on the steps of a country market down the road. A few moments passed before I noticed a man alongside me dressed in faded jeans and a patched shirt. His whiskered face, though crinkled with age, seemed tender. "You new here?" "No, just passing through. Visiting some forests." "Well, then, wait until fall. You haven't seen anything till you've watched those aspen turn golden."

In the fall, just as New England's brilliant foliage beckons thousands, so the turning of the aspen draws a stream of admirers to the Rockies. Quaking aspen—named for its fluttering leaves—ranks as North America's most widespread tree. Aspen is one of the few species in the largely evergreen forests of the Rockies to shed its foliage. About three-fourths of the aspen found in the Rocky Mountain states grows in Colorado, some three million acres in all.

Patches of red and gold aspen break the monotony of evergreen slopes. But aspen brings much more than beauty. It forms a natural firebreak; its fallen leaves enrich the soil so diverse plants can thrive in the understory; and it stabilizes the soil with its massive root systems. Aspen also provides food, cover, or nesting sites for some one hundred wildlife species.

For Colorado's aspen, however, the future is uncertain. Many of the stands are in decline—their root systems have lost vigor and cannot adequately reproduce. Without controlled clear-cutting, which stimulates regeneration, groves could begin disappearing within the next 20 years. But the threat of cutting trees as dear as these arouses much ire.

At the Fraser Experimental Forest near Fraser, Colorado, foresters have conducted aspen studies for several years. This 36-square-mile area, which lies within the Arapaho National Forest, was established by the Forest Service in 1937 as a research center for the subalpine woods. Project leader Robert R. Alexander is a silviculturist and author of some 90 technical papers. Having come to the experimental forest in 1950, Bob knows the woods of Colorado intimately. One cloudless day, he met me at Fraser.

As Bob talked, I found myself scrambling, changing tapes and flipping pages in my notebook. He explained that, unlike most species, aspen reproduces by cloning. Suckers—lateral roots—run underground and send up shoots to start new trees. A clone includes all the trees arising from a common root system. "In the fall, when you see one grove turned red and another yellow, each is a separate clone.

"While clear-cutting is effective in regenerating aspen groves," Bob said, "some aspens may not grow back after cutting. Snow piles in these clear-cuts and breaks off the young suckers, limiting regeneration." Bob added that fire can be effective in stimulating regeneration. Aspen often appears first on a burn site; through decades of fire suppression, however, other species have succeeded it in many places.

Bob told me that in 1984, Louisiana-Pacific opened a waferboard plant near Montrose, Colorado. Aspen waferboard, made of compressed chips, provides an alternative to plywood for paneling. Some see the company's operations, which involve cutting hundreds of acres annually, as a solution to the state's problem. Bob disagrees. "The company would probably prefer to cut the dense stands where the decline isn't great. Trees in those stands will usually regenerate. The aspens having problems regenerating," he emphasized, "are the individual trees and scattered plots. Those aspens are important visually and sometimes provide the only suitable habitat for certain animals in a coniferous area."

Later, as we drove through acres of evergreens crisscrossed by perky mountain streams, Bob told me about the experimental forest's ongoing studies to find ways to increase the yield of moisture from these high mountain watersheds. Water supply has long been a critical issue for the West and a poignant one for Colorado. Populous southern California draws much of its water from the Colorado River, whose headwaters rise just beyond Granby.

"If, for example, in high elevations, where snowfall is heaviest, we replace trees that use more water with those that require less moisture, we know we'll increase the runoff from those watersheds. Big water users like spruces and firs could be replaced with aspen and lodgepole pine. Of course, this isn't going to happen in my lifetime or yours. It's too costly, and we don't yet know what the impact would be on wildlife." Something to think about, though. The oceans may ensure us enough food, the forests, sufficient water.

As I pondered the valuable work being done by Bob and his staff, I recalled a remark made by one scientist at the Rocky Mountain Biological Laboratory. "What we are doing here," he told me, "is simple. We're reaffirming the bond between man and nature in a setting straight out of paradise." It was a comment that could apply equally well to many of the places I had visited.

Throughout the Rockies, woodlands endure—preserved in extensive national forests, parks, and wildernesses. In my journey alone, I passed through twelve national forests, four national parks, and seven wilderness areas.

Because these mountain forests are so extensive, it is easy to be lulled into believing they are eternal and immutable. They are not. Some are gone forever, others wounded by overlogging, disease, or the trampling of thoughtless visitors. What matters now is how we integrate our needs with those of the remaining forests. In doing so we will ensure that those who follow can discover for themselves what John Muir preached a century ago: "The clearest way into the Universe is through a forest wilderness."

ROCKY MOUNTAIN JUNIPER
Juniperus scopulorum

*F*ighting fire with fire, a crew in Montana's Helena National Forest checks an advancing blaze by igniting backfires. Eighteen wildfires struck Montana in August 1984, razing 225,770 acres. Though often devastating in the short term, fires help ensure the survival of many plant and animal species. Among their benefits, the blazes stimulate plant growth by opening the canopy and clearing the forest floor.

PRECEDING PAGES: Mirrored in a mountain lake, lightning streaks the sky above Wyoming's Wind River Range, imperiling forests parched by summer's scant rainfall. Such electrical storms spark most wildfires in the vast Rocky Mountain forests.

PAUL CHESLEY (134-5)

136

*N*o room for error means intense training for crew members of Helitack, a Canadian fire-fighting group. Near Oldman River in Alberta, two men practice rappelling from a helicopter; a spotter directs maneuvers from the chopper. Operating since 1978, Helitack now battles fires throughout the province, attempting to contain new blazes before they spread. The 70-member group successfully fought some 200 fires in 1984. Below, lodgepole pines cover a sunlit slope burned in 1936 along Dutch Creek, near Oldman River. Such hillsides offer evidence of ongoing forest succession: Lodgepole pines quickly claim burned-over areas, only to yield eventually to species such as spruce and fir.

FOLLOWING PAGES: *Defiant ranks of spruce and fir etch timberline at 7,000 feet on Thunder Mountain, in the Livingstone Range of the Canadian Rockies. While the tree line here rarely exceeds 6,500 feet, trees farther south often survive above 11,000 feet.*

N.G.S. PHOTOGRAPHER BRUCE DALE (BOTH AND 140-1)

*L*ike loggers of old, Jack Malmberg relies on horsepower to help thin a stand of lodgepole pine at Beaver Creek near Lander, Wyoming. Though more modern logging techniques prevail in most areas, horse logging works well for thinning such dense stands. These 60-to-80-year-old pines, stunted by inadequate light and moisture, find use mainly as firewood and fence posts. Below, at Montana's Lubrecht Experimental Forest near Missoula, cross sections from two 50-year-old pines illustrate one advantage of thinning operations: The bottom sample, grown among more widely spaced trees, more than doubles the top in size.

W̲ild wonderlands: Millions of acres of forested wilderness sustain a wealth of animal life in the Rockies. In Montana's Glacier National Park, a mountain goat (right) browses at the fringes of a subalpine woods; beyond juts 8,684-foot Bearhat Mountain. Summer brings grizzlies in search of food to higher elevations. With no enemies to fear other than man, a female and her cub (below) forage in Glacier Park near the North Fork of the Flathead River. Officials struggle to safeguard the grizzly—under federal protection since 1975. However, the expanding volume of visitors to the Rockies' backcountry threatens grizzly habitat, while increasing the likelihood of human-bear encounters.

TOM AND PAT LEESON (ABOVE); WILLIAM L. ALLEN, N.G.S. STAFF (RIGHT)

Morning mist softens the woods as a bull elk drinks from the Gibbon River in northwestern Wyoming, inside Yellowstone National Park. Up to 30,000 elk roam the park, migrating from lush mountain meadows to lower ground following September snows. Elk have long depended on Yellowstone and surrounding areas for grazing, especially in winter, when food is scarce. Herds of elk today range the Rockies from New Mexico to Canada.

Pocket of paradise, the 430-acre Mexican Cut Preserve in Colorado's Elk Mountains attracts scientists from nearby Rocky Mountain Biological Laboratory. Despite the remoteness of the largely untouched area, some fear it may suffer from such pollutants as acid rain. Over the past five summers, a team from the University of California at Berkeley has monitored the acid-buffering capacity of the preserve's numerous ponds. At right, a student takes an acidity reading of rainfall with a pH meter. The student below measures groundwater inflow to gauge the rate at which the pond can neutralize acid-bearing rain and snow.

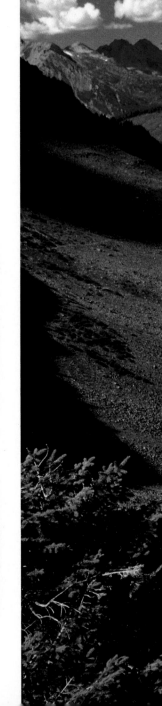

*S*howy *blooms of purple lupine crowd among aspen trees near Crested Butte, Colorado. Nitrogen absorbed into the soil from these common woodland plants helps promote vigorous growth in aspens. Curled amid shrubby cinquefoil and dandelions, the mule deer fawn at right will feed on the tender young shoots of aspen trees even while still nursing.*

PRECEDING PAGES: *In Idaho's Clearwater National Forest, the author camps along a portion of the hundred-mile Lolo Trail, a historic Indian route later followed by Lewis and Clark.*

*S*himmering with delicate colors, quaking aspens paint a woodland masterpiece in Colorado, where some three-fourths of the aspens in the U. S. Rockies grow. When aspens shed their leaves in fall (upper right), more sunlight reaches the forest floor (lower right). Buds that will grow into new aspens then form on the trees' roots. However, without periodic disturbances such as fires or clear-cuts, aspen stands may not regenerate. Conifers, able to tolerate more shade, often replace them.

FOLLOWING PAGES: Quaking aspens in autumn add vibrant swaths of gold to hillsides of evergreens in Uncompahgre National Forest, in Colorado.

PAUL CHESLEY (ALL AND 156-7)

*W*inter settles over Colorado's backcountry. At right, a cross-country ski instructor for the St. Paul Lodge slides past Engelmann spruce on Red Mountain. The lodge, a restored mine dating from the 1880s, perches just at timberline, here about 11,500 feet. In the tortuous terrain of the Highlands Bowl area (below), outside the popular resort town of Aspen, present regulations permit no skiing because of the persistent danger of avalanche.

Giants of the Pacific

By Merrill Windsor
Photographs by Paul Chesley

COAST REDWOOD
Sequoia sempervirens

I FIRST WROTE about the giant sequoias when I was in the fifth grade. "They are the biggest and oldest living things in the world," I declared confidently, summarizing what I'd read in the school library. "Some of them are more than 4,000 years old. In fact, the Gen. Sherman Tree is thought to be nearly 6,000 years old. These trees are in Calif."

For some reason my essay, abbreviations and all, was reproduced along with others in the town newspaper. Maybe it was national education week. With my statements engraved on the public record, I considered my facts unassailable. So it came as a shock when, nearly a quarter century later, in the late 1950s, I learned that bristlecone pines had replaced sequoias as the world's oldest known living things—and that the longevity of even the new champions fell considerably short of 6,000 years.

Now, driving toward Sequoia National Park in the Sierra Nevada, I wondered how much else that I learned in school had since come into question. We were told, for example, that the sequoia was named for Sequoyah, the Cherokee leader who devised an alphabet for the language of his people. Scholars now are not so sure. No matter. Whatever their age or the reason for their name, the wonder inspired by these largest of trees has not diminished.

Ten to twenty million years ago, before the Sierra Nevada thrust up to its present height, the ancestors of the giant sequoias covered parts of what is now southern Idaho and western Nevada. From there they slowly migrated to the south and west. As the great mountain range pushed skyward, its rain shadow left the land to the east too dry and warm for the big trees.

Today sequoias grow naturally only in a series of about 75 groves on the Sierra's western slopes, mainly at elevations of 5,000 to 7,500 feet, and within a strip less than 15 miles wide and about 260 miles long. Botanically, the trees are distinctive. Among their few close relatives are the coast redwoods of northern California's coastal fog belt and the dawn redwoods of central China.

Leaving the green fields and orchards of the San Joaquin Valley for the dusty foothills, I came to the Ash Mountain entrance to Sequoia National Park. Here, at an elevation of only 1,400 feet, chaparral shrubs and low oaks gave little hint of the soaring forest to come. But within a few miles the road began to twist and climb, opening vistas of jagged granite peaks to the east. Suddenly, at about 5,000 feet, I found myself in a cool woodland of pines, firs, and the huge, reddish brown trunks that could only mean giant sequoias.

At the Giant Forest—named by naturalist John Muir—I followed a path to the top of Moro Rock. The jutting monolith provides a sweeping view of forest, Sierra peaks, winding canyons, and the flat expanse of the great valley. That morning even the view upward was fascinating: An airy wisp of cloud refracted the sunlight in a delicate spectrum of color, as if a fragment had been snatched from a rainbow and tossed aloft to float alone in the blue summer sky.

Most of the sequoia groves scattered over their long range are relatively small and isolated. The greatest concentration

begins here at the Giant Forest and extends into adjacent Kings Canyon National Park. The Giant Forest contains many named trees, including the House and Senate Groups honoring the U. S. Congress. Here also is the monarch of sequoias, the General Sherman Tree— the largest known living thing on earth.

Nowhere are there extended pure stands of giant sequoias. The big trees share their surroundings with ponderosa and sugar pine, white fir, and incense cedar. The understory often includes California hazelnut, Pacific dogwood, and other shrubs and trees. Ground covers are scattered about, leaving much open forest floor. Even the low-growing plants can be attractions. The white blossoms of western azalea, for example, blaze flamboyantly along streams each spring.

Green meadows, bright with wildflowers, occasionally interrupt the woods. Emerging into a meadow strewn with orange leopard lilies, I gained a better perspective of the mammoth trees. The sequoias are so large that for years after their discovery in the mid-19th century, measurements of standing trees were only rough approximations. Accurate surveys made possible by modern instruments show the tallest sequoias stand about 310 feet high.

Calculating a sequoia's age is more complicated. Not for a felled tree, of course; an actual count of its annual growth rings is possible. (The highest confirmed count of a sequoia stump showed an age of 3,200 years.) No increment borer is long enough to penetrate the full radius of a mature living sequoia, so only partial cores can be taken. But, from a limited boring, scientists can now develop a growth-rate curve with which to estimate a given tree's age. Even so, they hedge their bets by several centuries. The official guess for General Sherman is 2,500 to 3,000 years.

We're fortunate that any of the sequoias survived for our enjoyment. The early years after their discovery were a time of laissez-faire attitudes and rapid commercial expansion in California. Entrepreneurs were intrigued with the thought of profits from trees so big that one could provide enough wood for 40 five-room houses. Indiscriminate harvesting began almost at once.

Several factors, however, limited the huge trees' desirability. Their size made them extremely difficult to cut down. Because they were so tall, and because their wood was brittle, the trees often shattered when they crashed to the ground. The brittleness of the wood made it of limited value in construction, and many of the trees ended up as grape stakes and shingles rather than as lumber. Even so, about a third of all the sequoias were destroyed between the 1850s and the 1950s, despite the gradual acquisition of groves for inclusion in national forests and state and national parks.

In the Redwood Mountain Grove of Kings Canyon National Park, I followed a trail that climbed steadily through the big trees. I had to pause every few minutes to catch my breath. Once I was standing in silence when, perhaps a hundred yards away, I saw a blur of motion, then heard a tremendous crash followed by resounding echoes. Although there was no wind, a great sequoia branch—as big as a good-size pine—had broken loose and fallen to the earth.

If a *branch* can cause that much noise, I thought, what would the falling of a sequoia tree be like? Entire sequoias do sometimes crash to the ground, not just during a storm but even on a still day. These great trees have no permanent taproots; their root systems are broad but shallow, and if one finally loses its balance, there is nothing to anchor it.

As I hiked on, I suddenly realized I was entirely surrounded by giants—every tree in view was a sequoia. Picking a soft, leafy spot, I lay flat on my back and looked up at the circle of arching branches far above, watching them sway in the light breeze. Across the patch of blue sky moved a billowy cloud tinged with gray, and I wished for a moment for the drama of a Sierra thunderstorm. Almost all this forest's 40 to 50 inches of yearly precipitation comes in the form of heavy winter snows, but occasional summer rainstorms moisten the soil and sweeten the air.

But the cloud passed on, and I focused again on the distant treetops. When I was young I used to lie within a ring of ponderosa pines and stare upward, hoping no one would call me to chores. In those days I thought the pines were big!

From the world's largest living trees, I set out to visit the oldest. Bristlecone pines have been recognized as the most venerable of trees only since the 1950s. When dendrochronologist Edmund Schulman of the University of Arizona hunted down the Great Basin bristlecones to study their growth rings, he found several more than 4,000 years old. Shortly before his death in 1958, Schulman discovered the pine he dubbed Methuselah. Its age then was 4,600.

Crossing the Sierra Nevada at Tioga Pass, I dropped to the trough of the Owens Valley and then started climbing toward the Ancient Bristlecone Pine Forest in the White Mountains. The bristlecone pine region, protected within the Inyo National Forest, is set aside for scientific research and public enjoyment.

The rising road wound through sagebrush foothills, up to junipers and piñons, then into desert scrub before it came to scattered limber pines and the first of the ancient trees. Here most other vegetation fell away, for the upper elevations of the White Mountains are anything but hospitable to plants: shallow limestone soil; limited precipitation (about ten inches annually); desiccating heat in summer; bitter cold in winter; high winds during parts of the year.

Stopping at Schulman Memorial Grove, I noticed an obvious difference between north-facing and south-facing slopes. Cynthia Horwitz, a seasonal interpreter at the Forest Service's trailer-turned-visitor-center, explained.

"On the north-facing slopes, the winter snows linger, and their slow melt doles out the moisture. That not only increases the numbers and growth rate of the bristlecones but also supports organisms that attack living trees and speed decomposition of deadwood.

"In contrast, the vegetation on the southern slopes is much more sparse, and the trees are more stunted and twisted. On such dry mountainsides, they grow more slowly and their wood is highly resinous. It resists decay and insects, and the trees often live much longer."

Even when the trees finally die, Cynthia added, many remain standing for centuries, and when they fall they may lie in a preserved state for thousands of years, since fire here is rare and in any case would have difficulty spreading on such barren slopes. This ancient deadwood has made it possible for Dr. Schulman's colleague and successor in research, C. W. Ferguson, to push back the record of tree-ring chronology. Schulman traced the record of climatic change for the past 4,600 years by examining the growth rings of living trees. Dr. Ferguson has gradually extended the record another 4,000 years by matching overlapping growth ring patterns from living trees with those of older wood remnants.

Exploring the grove, I followed a short trail past contorted forms that included—unidentified—Pine Alpha, the first bristlecone Schulman found that was more than 4,000 years old. The tree is not singled out, to protect it from the unwanted attention of souvenir hunters.

"Gaunt runts," one writer has called these strange plants, few of which reach more than 25 feet high on the drier sites. The description is accurate as far as it goes, but it does not acknowledge the trees' almost eerie beauty, reminiscent of an exotic bonsai. "Living driftwood," wrote another. Yet only part living, and therein lies the secret.

The bristlecone pine sustains life for dozens of centuries by adapting its needs to almost impossible conditions and, in the most difficult times, even partially suspending growth for short periods. The living branches are supplied by a narrow strip of sapwood nurtured by cambial tissue. These form a lifeline from the roots to the foot-long concentrations of short needles at the ends of the branches. Each scale of the female cones ends in a prickly bristle—hence the tree's name.

Except for the bristlecones and an occasional grass clump or wildflower, the mountainside was barren. Here and there dolomite outcroppings broke the angle of the slope, and talus slides of flat brown sandstone covered half a hillside. Rain clouds were lowering, but I was determined to see the forest's greatest stand of ancient trees, reached by the four-mile Methuselah Walk.

I kept as brisk a pace as I could manage at this unaccustomed elevation—10,100 feet. Cynthia had given me a pamphlet keyed to numbered posts, with commentary on plants, animals, terrain, and climate. At one station a cross section of a bristlecone pine had been positioned for easy viewing and marked at the ring representing the year of Christ's birth. The pamphlet pointed out that many of these trees had been alive throughout most of recorded history—and the oldest were already several centuries old when Egypt's Great Pyramid was completed!

I was fascinated by the persistence of these stubborn plants, their gnarled and twisted forms, and the sculptural quality of the white wood, eroded and polished by wind-borne particles of sand and ice.

Somewhere I passed the Methuselah Tree without knowing which it was. Like Pine Alpha, it is not identified. But even Methuselah is not the oldest recorded bristlecone. In 1964 a 4,900-year-old tree was found in the mountains of east-central Nevada, though it has since died.

The rain held off until I had begun the 12-mile drive farther up the mountain to the Patriarch Grove. Beyond the Schulman Grove the landscape became desert scrub again, and cattle grazed in accord with the Forest Service's multiple-use policy. A pudgy marmot edged off a low boulder at roadside and went looking for drier quarters.

In August there were wildflowers growing here. I saw the vermilion of Indian paintbrush, the violet-blue of lupine, small white daisies. The rain turned to light mist that glistened on the blossoms. By the time I reached my goal, at an elevation of just over 11,000 feet, the ground was an austere slope of fragmented white rock, from which the irregular shapes of bristlecones rose as if set out on display by some extravagant sculptor.

The principal attraction of the grove, a mix of old and young trees, is the largest known bristlecone pine—the Patriarch, an imposing, multistemmed tree that is more than 36 feet in circumference. In age, however, it is not even an elder—not quite 1,500 years old.

I started back down the mountain in a full-fledged summer downpour. Just as I reached the lookout point at Sierra View, the sun broke through to illuminate part of the Owens Valley and the crest of the Sierra. Then the clouds closed in again, and I left the bristlecones to another of the countless storms they have endured down through the centuries.

"Let me tell you about the red tree vole project," said Kate Barrows. "The red what?" I asked. "The red tree vole. That's a mouselike species that lives in the tops of tall trees, especially Douglas firs."

In the Barrows' pickup truck, Kate and her husband, Cameron, and I were bouncing along the shady, curving dirt road that runs deep into the Northern California Coast Range Preserve near Branscomb, California. Cam and Kate are the managers of this unusual cooperative effort, which encompasses 4,000 acres owned by the private Nature Conservancy and 4,000 belonging to the Bureau of Land Management. Mostly virgin forest, the preserve was established 26 years ago and is the oldest Nature Conservancy project in the western United States.

The land was set aside for general ecological research and education through nonexperimental programs—"There's little active manipulation of the environment here," Cam explained—while keeping the area accessible for recreational use. Under a reservation system, visitors come here to hike, swim, picnic, and observe wildlife.

The BLM designated its part of the property as a research natural area and provided funds for fire management studies. The Forest Service sponsors studies of this old-growth woodland as a wildlife habitat. The U. S. Geological Survey has a hydrologic benchmark station on Elder Creek, which drains much of the area.

Investigations by researchers—principally university faculty members and graduate students—cover a wide range in subject and magnitude, lasting anywhere from a couple of weekends to six months or a year of full-time effort. The red tree vole figured in one of these studies.

"Apparently it lives most of its life in the trees and rarely comes down to the ground," Kate said. "It seems to travel considerable distances to get its nesting material, but we think it stays upstairs, moving from branch to branch and tree to tree. Anyway, a young woman is coming to do a definitive study."

I asked the obvious question. "How does she get up there to observe these aerial mice?"

"She's a very gutsy lady," Kate said. "She's been learning to use climbing irons—just like telephone linemen use to climb poles."

The Coast Range Preserve is primarily mixed evergreen forest, containing not only conifers—Douglas fir, coast redwood, some sugar and ponderosa pine— but also broadleaf evergreens such as madrona, tan oak, and canyon live oak. In places oaks predominate, especially on south- and west-facing slopes.

The Barrows were hired by the Conservancy four years ago. Kate had been a park naturalist in southern California; Cam had been studying spotted owls and their natural habitat. Both knew this area intimately, having first come here on field assignments while students at the University of California at Davis. At the Barrows' house I later admired some of the pen-and-ink drawings Cam has done of the northern spotted owl—a species designated as "sensitive" but not yet endangered. "This is the ideal place to study them," Cam said. "Spotted owls need old-growth forest, and of course there isn't much left."

I asked how these unlogged forests happened to be available to the Nature Conservancy as recently as 1959. "A couple named Heath and Marjorie Angelo had started buying up land around here years ago," Kate said. "They wanted to try to keep it in its natural state. When Mr. Angelo sold the land, he arranged with the Conservancy to live here, and he stayed on until he died. He was a marvelous old gentleman; if you went to call on him, he always served George Dickel whiskey and chocolate chip cookies. He loved it here, and he knew a lot about the plants and animals."

Elder Creek flows into the South Fork of the Eel River, which itself passes through the heart of the preserve. Crossing a narrow bridge over the creek, we looked down at the transparent water. "Even in times of heavy rainfall, the water remains clear," Cam said, "because

PACIFIC DOGWOOD
Cornus nuttallii

there's been no logging upstream. The Elder Creek watershed is the largest in northwestern California that has not been logged. Its entire ecological system has been protected." As a result, the watershed has been designated a national natural landmark.

One recreational activity restricted in the preserve is fishing. Salmon and steelhead use the South Fork and Elder Creek as spawning grounds, and one of the research projects is a comparative study to determine the effects of logging operations on salmon and steelhead reproduction.

Here and there we passed a tall redwood. One had been hit by lightning. Its top was a naked spire. "This is just about the inland limit of the redwoods' range," Cam said. "The coastal mountains hold back the fog, so it's a bit too warm and dry for them here."

The coast redwood prefers the cool, moist strip of low mountains and protected valleys paralleling the Pacific from just south of the Monterey Peninsula to just north of the Oregon border. Shielded from ocean winds and salt air by the first tier of coastal heights, the 500-mile-long fog belt extends inland an average of 20 miles. Here the annual rainfall of 60 to 120 inches comes almost entirely in winter. But the dry summer months are moderated by frequent fog that protects the great trees from excessive transpiration.

This mild realm was left to the redwoods by the glaciers of the last ice age, which elsewhere destroyed the trees over a vast area. A century and a half ago, just before the logger's ax and saw arrived, the entire fog belt supported a nearly uninterrupted redwood forest of some two million acres. Perhaps a tenth of that virgin growth survives today.

The magnificent coast redwoods are the world's tallest known living things, many of them growing 300 to 350 feet high. (The tallest tree, discovered in 1963 by a National Geographic Society team, measured 367.8 feet.) Although the great

WESTERN RED CEDAR
Thuja plicata

trees dominate their habitat, they often share it with other conifers—Douglas fir, western hemlock, Sitka spruce—and with such trees as tan oak, madrona, big-leaf maple, and red alder. But in the most favorable circumstances, usually along sheltered streamside terraces, redwoods sometimes occur in nearly pure stands. The beauty of these groves of soaring, symmetrical giants is legendary, their tapered crowns reaching toward the clouds while at their feet cluster colonies of shade-tolerant shrubs, ferns, and flowers.

Although the redwood forest was far more extensive than the scattered sequoia groves of the Sierra Nevada, it came even closer than they to being wiped out by logging. There were two main reasons: The wood made excellent lumber, much more useful and versatile than the brittle sequoia wood; and the coast redwoods grew closer to convenient shipping points, which provided wider marketing opportunities.

As with the giant sequoias, public interest first stirred a century or more ago to preserve these trees. But whereas the federal government moved relatively early to protect the sequoias by creating national parks, the effort to defend the coast redwoods remained essentially one of state and private agencies—inspired after 1918 by the indefatigable Save-the-Redwoods League. Not until 1968 did Congress finally establish Redwood National Park to augment the northernmost state parks; a second act ten years later added other redwood groves and the protective buffer of additional watershed land.

Today there are significant redwood preserves at intervals throughout the trees' historic range, but the greatest concentration begins north of Fort Bragg and continues almost to Oregon. In this 200-mile stretch are more than a dozen redwood state parks, preserves, and recreation areas, the last three linked by the new national park.

The giant trees create a shadowy,

mysterious setting unlike any other I've known. Heading northward from Fort Bragg, I prowled dim corridors among the redwoods, hiking the quiet forest trails. In Humboldt Redwoods State Park, I followed a trail along Bull Creek from the Big Tree Area to Bull Creek Flats. Even on a sunny day the forest floor, quite open here, was bathed in soft, filtered light. Oxalis carpeted the hollows with its large, clover-shaped leaves. In places the path was bordered with luxuriant gardens of bracken, sword, or lady ferns.

Among the trunks of mature trees rose the seedlings and saplings of new generations. Unlike most other conifers, coast redwoods reproduce not only by seed but also by sprouts that spring from the burls at the bases of trees. With the advantage of established roots, these youngsters usually grow much faster than seedlings. One reason for the relatively rapid regeneration of cutover redwood forest is the frequent sprouting from the stumps of felled trees.

A shaft of sunlight pierced the canopy to spotlight the perky pink blossoms of wild rose. Just beyond was another of the forest's many fallen trees, the wheel of its shallow root system turned on edge. From the remains of another fallen trunk rose a fountain of ferns and small flowering plants, giving the effect of an oversize, untended window box.

At Bull Creek Flats I gazed at the splendid old trees of Rockefeller Forest. On average, coast redwoods live about 500 to 800 years, but some last much longer. The stump of the oldest known redwood shows it was 2,200 years old when cut. Many of the trees in Rockefeller Forest are thought to be more than a thousand years old.

Next day, as I neared Prairie Creek Redwoods State Park, I realized I had noticed little wildlife among the tall trees. Scurrying chickarees and gray squirrels, of course, and a few blue streaks in the soft light as jays flashed from branch to shrub. But I had detected no sign of the bears, deer, and bobcats known to frequent parts of the coastal forest.

I was soon to be compensated. On both sides of the highway ahead, dozens of cars had pulled off. People had gathered along a fence overlooking a long meadow. The attraction was a herd of perhaps 40 Roosevelt elk grazing just beyond the barrier.

The elk have the entire park in which to roam, but this day they had considerately wandered close enough to the road for all to see. California's largest land animals, the elk were nearing extinction in the early part of this century. Now they are protected and have made a strong comeback. As we watched, the regal animals drifted away, indifferent to the pleasure they had given us.

Everything was wet. Not soaked, just wet. My jacket, my boots, the trail ahead, every rock, branch, and trunk I could see. From the trees overhead came a steady drip-drip-drip onto my head. It all seemed appropriate, for this was Washington's Hoh River Valley, and I had come to see the rain forests of Olympic National Park.

It doesn't rain here all the time, the rangers assured me. But there are two cloudy or rainy days for every sunny one (most of the latter kind come in summer), and the annual precipitation in the three adjacent rain forest valleys—Hoh, Queets, Quinault—averages 145 inches. Laden with moisture from the Pacific Ocean, clouds move eastward across the coastline of northern Washington only to be blocked by the Olympic Mountains. A few of the highest clouds clear the barrier; the rest shed rain on the ridges and valleys of the western slopes or drop snow on the spectacular peaks and ice fields of the central range.

The Hoh, Queets, and Quinault get a generous supply of Pacific fog, along with snow-fed runoff from the Olympics. The constant saturation, combined with mild temperatures and the fine-textured soil of the wide, almost flat valley floors, has made them one of the continent's most favorable environments for luxuriant plant growth. The result is a classic temperate rain forest of amazing density and variety.

The kings of the rain forest are 200-foot-tall Sitka spruces, attended by western hemlocks and Douglas fir. Red alders, black cottonwoods, and bigleaf maples grow near the conifer canopy, usually along lower river terraces. Shrubs and small trees, including tangles of vine maple, make up the understory. Grasses, ferns, mosses, and wildflowers mantle the ground. And almost everywhere—but especially on the bigleaf maples—appear the curious plants called epiphytes, such as club moss and licorice fern. The epiphytes attach themselves to other plants but take nothing from their hosts, drawing their sustenance solely from airborne nutrients and moisture.

Sometimes heavy rains fall here, particularly in winter; but generally the precipitation is a drizzle that is diffused by high foliage and gradually drips its way to earth. Even on clear, sunny days, the rain forest retains its cool dampness and distinctive smell, combining the fragrance of fresh new growth and the mustiness of moldering humus.

I was contemplating a line of young hemlocks not far from the Hoh Visitor Center when I noticed that the steady dripping had stopped and a sunbeam was groping through the treetops. Turning onto another path, I overtook a group of raincoated visitors accompanied by a tall, personable naturalist named Bob Larson.

Rather than ramble through a memorized commentary, Bob involved his audience at every pause along the trail. Someone asked about tree identification—how to tell Sitka spruce from western hemlock. "Everyone take hold of one of these branchlets," Bob said. "Run your hand lightly upward against the needles. Feel how sharp and prickly they are? That's spruce—every spruce has that kind of sharp, stiff needle. And look at the branch, end on. See how the needles come out all around the twig? Now look at this tree's soft, lacy spray of foliage. Feel it. That's western hemlock." And so it went, stop by stop.

Senior naturalist Walt Chance and his staff handled a heavy volume of visitor traffic at the Hoh center with efficiency and good humor. Displays prepare newcomers for a network of well-maintained trails, from short, self-guiding nature walks to backpacking routes reaching into the Olympic high country. For two days I sampled the trails of the Hoh, then I went next door to the adjacent valley on the north, to compare what author-naturalist Ruth Kirk calls the "almost" rain forest of the Bogachiel River Valley.

The distinctions between the Bogachiel and the Hoh are technical, but significant to those who study and classify prime rain forest. The Hoh, Queets, and Quinault Valleys—gouged out by glaciers—are U-shape in cross section. The Bogachiel, though also glaciated, takes more of the conventional stream-cut V shape. Because the valley is not as broad, its soils are different, and it therefore contains a somewhat altered combination of the plants found in the Hoh. Notably, Douglas fir rather than Sitka spruce has become the most prevalent species in the Bogachiel.

There are other subtle differences of importance to science, but for the layman hiker the two valleys are equally beautiful, equally exciting—and equally damp. I found one selfish advantage in the relatively inaccessible Bogachiel. For the seeker of solitude, it offers a true wilderness environment. I tramped through its groves and vales for hours without encountering another human being.

The scene here was ever changing, and surprises were frequent. Thick undergrowth gave way abruptly to open glens where browsing elk had, in places, all but cleared away the salmonberry and other shrubs. Elsewhere curtains of hanging

moss completely veiled one side of the trail; then the passage opened into an airy glade lined by red alders, their trunks splotched whitish gray by lichens, their light leaves dancing in sunlight high overhead.

Leafy ground covers were punctuated with yellow buttercups. A bright orange fungus made startling contrast with the dark brown snag on which it was growing. Vine maples arched randomly above the path. The forest, silent except for my own breathing, suddenly filled with birdsong. Later the lyrical sound of a hillside waterfall gave way to the roar of rapids as I neared the Bogachiel River.

It was the elk of the Hoh Valley that gave me a final send-off from these lush forests. As I got into my car on my last afternoon here, two calves wandered from the trees and out onto the asphalt. One stopped, but the other came on—right up to my window. If I'd had room, I'm sure he would have accepted a ride.

Here in the Pacific Northwest, one can still see stirring evidence of the relation of woodlands to the arts and crafts of Native Americans. In dramatic totem poles, in great war canoes, in a variety of ornamental and utilitarian wood carvings, the Northwest Coast Indians traditionally used both the trees and the motifs provided by nature. During the first half of this century their skills were almost lost, but in recent decades there has been a renaissance of interest and involvement in that tradition.

One of the influential artists and teachers is himself not an Indian. Duane Pasco grew up in Alaska and Washington and was encouraged to develop his artistic aptitude while in high school. "I guess I've always been interested in Indian culture," Duane told me, "and the fact that art plays such an important role in it." His earliest creative efforts were pencil portraits, but in the 1960s he started carving and painting in the style of the Northwest Coast Indian. "That really fascinated me," he said. "The bold style has a discipline that appeals to me."

In 1969 there was a growing need for teachers for the training schools and cultural centers that were opening as a result of resurging interest in Northwest Coast art. Pasco's work was so respected that he was welcomed as a teacher and adviser by the Native Americans. Since then he has divided his time between teaching and a prolific output in media ranging from painting and silk-screening to a wide variety of sculpture, including ceremonial masks, bas-relief panels, and totem poles. Some of his major works are on permanent display at the Seattle-Tacoma International Airport.

At their home in the woods near Poulsbo, Washington, Duane and his wife and business manager, Katie, let me wander through their living and family rooms and the spacious studio. The whole place was a gallery, displaying not only Duane's work but also pieces by other artists. Duane was just beginning a distinctive bas-relief on a large, curved panel. As in much of his work, the dominant theme was birth, represented in this design by the red-tailed hawk.

The same wood Duane Pasco was using, western red cedar, was Calvin Hunt's choice for the totem pole he was carving when I found him at work in Fort Rupert, a Kwakiutl Indian community near the northern end of Vancouver Island, in British Columbia. The pole, laid out in his new workshop, was taking shape: The thunderbird at top and killer whale below were already formed; the lower designs were roughed out. In another six weeks the finished totem pole, 31 feet tall and 34 inches in diameter, would be on display in the new IBM Corporation office building in Manhattan. After its three-month sojourn there it was destined for New York's Museum of the American Indian.

The modest, 29-year-old Hunt had moved back to Fort Rupert after spending much of his life in Victoria. There, from age 15, he had studied sculpture with his older cousin, Tony Hunt, and Tony's father, Henry Hunt, probably the best known and most highly regarded contemporary Northwest Coast Indian artists.

Calvin explained the significance of the pole's elements. "The thunderbird is on the alert, watching over the people. The killer whale is their protector. At the bottom, a chief wearing his blanket represents wealth. A large crest pole like this would stand at the house of a chief."

Driving the length of Vancouver Island to Fort Rupert and back was a scenic pleasure. In turn came beaches, green hills, neat Mennonite farms, towns landscaped with countless flower beds. Then the verdant farmlands gave way to thickly forested mountains and an occasional lake. The heights were crowned with white mist and some, even in August, with snow. I shared the road with few other cars. Stalks of spectacular lavender fireweed brightened the grassy roadside.

The only jarring notes were provided by the periodic appearance of a freshly logged mountainside. The journey made it clear why lumbering ranks as one of British Columbia's main industries. Block cutting is the rule in these vast stands of Douglas fir and western hemlock. In geometric rectangles a tract is clear-cut, while strips of mature trees are left standing on two or more sides, according to terrain. These strips provide corridors for wildlife and help control fire by breaking the continuity of slash so a blaze's spread is slowed.

Clear-cutting is, of course, the most economical way to harvest the trees. One can understand the practice yet still be saddened by the sight of a recently ravaged slope. I thought the British Columbia Ministry of Forests could have placed one of its fire prevention signboards more judiciously. Directly overlooking a newly logged vale, it read: "Thank you for keeping our forests green."

There are numerous provincial parks and forest reserves on Vancouver Island.

As my final stop, I visited a unique section of MacMillan Provincial Park called Cathedral Grove. It is a dense stand of old-growth forest dominated by huge Douglas firs. The grove contains at least three other coniferous species—western red cedar, western hemlock, and grand fir—as well as the deciduous bigleaf maple.

"Look well!" exclaimed a welcoming panel. "Here are the last of the big trees along major roads of southern British Columbia. Once there were many groves like this."

About 300 years ago a fire swept through this woodland, clearing the undergrowth, opening up the forest, and providing—in combination with the valley's fertile soils and damp sea air—ideal growing conditions. Today some of the trees are 800 years old, the largest reaching 246 feet high. Fallen logs are abundant, and several form footbridges across streams and dry creek beds.

Deep dusk came early to Cathedral Grove. Next morning the overcast sky sent a gentle, pervasive light into the forest. For several hours I roamed its trails. At noon, perhaps predictably on verdant Vancouver Island, it started to rain. I finished reading a bronze plaque dedicated to David Douglas, the young botanist who wandered the fields and forests of the Pacific coast in the first third of the 19th century. The Douglas fir perpetuates his name.

The rain increased, but it didn't matter now. It was time to leave. As I took a long, last look at this tranquil sanctuary, I reflected on my exploration of the Pacific forests. My experience had been as humbling as it was instructive. Each ecological province I had visited, from the arid bristlecone pine slopes to the luxuriant rain forest, had demonstrated the same enduring principle: the wondrous complexity of relationships to be found throughout nature. It was a truth I'd known all along, of course, but one that blossomed afresh midst the peace and beauty of these wild woodlands.

GIANT SEQUOIA
Sequoiadendron giganteum

Land of superlatives, the Far West boasts the world's oldest, largest, and tallest trees. The oldest: the Great Basin bristlecone pines, found in greatest numbers in Inyo National Forest (left), in California. Some have survived more than 4,000 years. Here, Dr. C. W. Ferguson of the University of Arizona and Forest Service volunteer David Pomaville prepare to take a core sample from a bristlecone with an increment borer. The sample will enable them to determine the tree's age. Near the tips of branches grow young purplish male cones (below and right) and an older, larger female cone (right).

PAGES 172-173: Ancient bristlecone pine lives on, as shown by the foliage to the left of the trunk.

lames of a prescribed burn consume the litter of the forest floor in California's Sequoia National Park. Below, members of the control crew monitor the burn in a stand of white fir. At bottom, torches ignite debris at the base of a giant sequoia, whose fire-resistant bark bears the blackened scars of earlier wildfires. Fire plays a critical role in sequoia reproduction, preparing the soil and helping in distribution and germination of seed. At right, a giant smoke ring encircles a sequoia trunk.

PAGES 178-179: *Blazing staghorn lichens turn tall white firs into pillars of fire. The dry lichens burn quickly, leaving the trees singed but usually unharmed.*

*R*eturning its organic matter to the soil, a fallen tree decays amid sedge and lavender shooting stars in Sequoia National Park, named for the largest known living things. Giant sequoia trees grow naturally only in some 75 scattered groves on the western slopes of the Sierra Nevada. In Kings Canyon National Park, a persistent scarlet monkey flower (top left) emerges from a crack in a cut log. Numerous other flowering plants, including leopard lily (lower left), brighten trailsides and meadows in Sequoia and adjacent Kings Canyon.

Surrounded by sword and lady ferns, ranger Jim Burke measures the girth of the Dyerville Giant in Humboldt Redwoods State Park, in northern California. Coast redwoods reign as the world's tallest trees, some reaching 350 feet or more in height. The redwoods flourish in a 500-mile-long fog belt extending from just south of the Monterey Peninsula to just north of the Oregon border. Although not the tallest redwood, the Dyerville Giant takes the title for overall size, its trunk some 52 feet in circumference. Below, plant ecologist Mary Hektner examines a Douglas fir seedling planted on once logged-over land now part of Redwood National Park. Straw mulch helps control erosion.

FOLLOWING PAGES: Salt-tolerant Sitka spruces top sea cliffs north of California's Klamath River, shielding inland redwoods.

Northern spotted owl peers from a branch of a tan oak tree in the Northern California Coast Range Preserve. This 8,000-acre forest contains a mix of old-growth conifers and broadleaf evergreens, ideal habitat for spotted owls. Below, a bird-watcher scans the high branches of redwood trees near a trail in Redwood National Park. Established in 1968, the California sanctuary augments numerous redwood state parks, preserves, and recreation areas.

Sunlight burns through the fog of Del Norte Coast Redwoods State Park, illuminating the large blossoms of California rosebay, a type of rhododendron. Curly-tipped sword ferns thrust up below the flowering shrubs. Although most rainfall along the northern California coast comes in winter, fog occurs throughout the summer, supplying redwoods and associated plants with the high humidity they need. At Founders Grove in Humboldt Redwoods State Park (below), carpets of oxalis, or wood sorrel—probably the most common ground cover in the redwood forest—flank a half-mile, self-guiding trail. The grove honors the founders of the Save-the-Redwoods League, an organization that has fought to preserve redwoods since 1918.

Stroller in a rain forest in Washington's Olympic National Park pauses to feel the soft texture of mosses. Here also grow club mosses, plants more closely allied to ferns. From the side of a Sitka spruce (opposite, top), wood sorrel puts forth its bright green leaves and white blossoms. At left, a chickaree, or Douglas squirrel, collects a cone to store away.

FOLLOWING PAGES: Roots of western hemlocks embrace a rotting log in Cathedral Grove, on Vancouver Island, British Columbia. In the wet forests along the Pacific coast, seedlings often germinate in the rich beds of such fallen, decaying trees, called nurse logs.

Tender fingers touch the craggy bark of a forest elder in Cathedral Grove. Part of MacMillan Provincial Park, the grove preserves a dense stand of old-growth forest. Here huge Douglas firs, some 800 years old, dominate. Throughout North America, the grandeur of such wild forest realms continues to enthrall visitors of all ages.

Notes on Contributors

Photographer PAUL CHESLEY contributes regularly to NATIONAL GEO-GRAPHIC and has covered the Four Corners area, Death Valley, the Saw-tooth Range, and the natural splendors of Europe for Special Publications. Paul, who lives in Aspen, Colorado, photographed the Society's book *High Country Trail: Along the Continental Divide*.

Formerly with *Southern Living*, photographer MIKE CLEMMER has com-pleted several assignments for Special Publications and WORLD maga-zine. His photographs also have appeared in *Newsweek*, *Time*, *USA Today*, and other magazines and newspapers. Born in North Carolina, Mike now lives with his wife in Birmingham, Alabama.

A professor of American studies at Princeton University, WILLIAM HOWARTH has written four stories for NATIONAL GEOGRAPHIC and a chapter in the Society's *Great Rivers of the World*. He is the author or edi-tor of ten books, including two that deal in part with forest ecology, *The Book of Concord* and *Thoreau in the Mountains*.

Photographer STEVEN C. KAUFMAN has completed assignments for the Special Publication *Wild Lands for Wildlife* and for TRAVELER magazine. A former seasonal park ranger, Steven specializes in natural history pho-tography, with a preference for northern latitudes and the wildlife found there. He lives in Homer, Alaska.

JANE R. McCAULEY lived three years in Geneva, Switzerland, before joining the Society's staff in 1970. Her writing credits include two Books for Young Explorers—*Ways Animals Sleep* and *Baby Birds and How They Grow*—and chapters in the Special Publications *Secret Corners of the World* and *Exploring America's Valleys*.

A graduate of Howard University, H. ROBERT MORRISON joined the So-ciety's staff in 1964. His many contributions to Special Publications in-clude chapters in *Mysteries of the Ancient World*, *Preserving America's Past*, and *America's Hidden Corners*. Bob is the coauthor of the Special Publication *America's Atlantic Isles*.

Painter, illustrator, and writer ALAN SINGER heads his own studio, Sandpiper Art & Design, in Brooklyn, New York. In 1980, the U. S. Postal Service commissioned Alan and his father, Arthur Singer, to paint a series of 50 stamps illustrating the official bird and flower of every state. The hardcover illustration for this book is taken from that series.

TIM THOMPSON, who began his career as a writer, became a full-time photographer in 1972. His photographs have appeared in *Time-Life* books, *Audubon*, and various airline magazines. Tim contributed to the Special Publications *Alaska's Magnificent Parklands* and *Exploring Ameri-ca's Valleys*. He lives on Bainbridge Island, near Seattle, Washington.

JENNIFER C. URQUHART, a native of the Washington, D. C., area, grad-uated from Smith College. A Society staff member since 1973, she has written chapters for *America's Wild and Scenic Rivers* and *Exploring Amer-ica's Scenic Highways*. Jenny has contributed to TRAVELER magazine and is the author of the children's book *Animals That Travel*.

A former Rhodes scholar, MERRILL WINDSOR recently returned to his native Arizona after serving as managing editor of *Sunset* magazine, then spending 13 years as an editor with the Society. He has since undertaken writing assignments for TRAVELER magazine and *Arizona Highways*. Merrill is the author of the Special Publication *America's Sunset Coast*.

Additional Reading

The reader may wish to consult the *National Geographic Index* for perti-nent articles, and to refer to the following: Liberty Hyde Bailey and Ethel Zoe Bailey, *Hortus Third: A Concise Dictionary of Plants Cultivated in the United States and Canada*; Robert G. Bailey, *Description of the Ecoregions of the United States*; Richard C. Davis, editor, *Encyclopedia of American Forest and Conservation History*, vols. 1 and 2; Thomas S. Elias, *The Complete Trees of North America*; F. H. Eyre, editor, *Forest Cover Types of the United States and Canada*; Michael Frome, *The Forest Service*; R. C. Hosia, *Native Trees of Canada*; Elbert L. Little, *The Audubon Society Field Guide to North American Trees*, Eastern and Western Regions.

HARALD SUND

Index

Illustration references appear in **boldface**.

Library of Congress CIP Data
Main entry under title:
America's wild woodlands.
  Bibliography: p.
  Includes index.
  1. Forest ecology—United States.
2. Forests and forestry—United States.
3. Forest reserves—United States.
I. National Geographic Society (U.S.).
Special Publications Division.
QH104.A748 1985 917.3'0915'2 85-355
ISBN 0-87044-542-1 (regular edition)
ISBN 0-87044-547-2 (library edition)

Acknowledgments

Chickadee & White Pine Cone and Tassel

The Special Publications Division is grateful to the individuals, groups, and organizations named and quoted in the text and to those cited here for their assistance during the preparation of this book: Rudolf W. Becking, Robert Belous, Robert Bodine, Richard R. Buech, W. L. Davidson, Jr., John D. Freeman, Bill Gardiner, Joseph W. Gorsh, Donald D. Grant, Ralph Gray, Tom H. Hooper, Frances A. Hunt, Walter D. Kelly, Elbert L. Little, John David McFarland III, Brian Miller, Judd Moore, John J. Palmer, Ed Schreiner, Susan F. Schafer, Dave Steeinke, Harold K. Steen, A. Keith Strange, Steve Tim. Special thanks to the Postal Service for permission to reproduce the artwork at left on the hard cover. Painted by Arthur and Alan Singer, stamp is from the series commemorating the birds and flowers of the 50 states. Copyright © 1982, U.S. Postal Service.

Composition for *America's Wild Woodlands* by National Geographic's Photographic Services, Carl M. Shrader, Director, Lawrence F. Ludwig, Assistant Director. Printed and bound by Holladay-Tyler Printing Corp., Rockville, Md. Film preparation by Catharine Cooke Studio, Inc., New York, N.Y. Color separations by the Lanman Progressive Company, Washington, D. C.; Lincoln Graphics, Inc., Cherry Hill, N.J.; and NEC, Inc., Nashville, Tenn.